Faculty Job Satisfaction:
Women and Minorities in Peril

by Martha Wingard Tack and Carol Logan Patitu

ASHE-ERIC Higher Education Report No. 4, 1992

Prepared by

Clearinghouse on Higher Education
The George Washington University

In cooperation with

Association for the Study
of Higher Education

Published by

School of Education and Human Development
The George Washington University

Jonathan D. Fife, Series Editor

Cite as

Tack, Martha Wingard, and Carol Logan Patitu. 1992. *Faculty Job Satisfaction: Women and Minorities in Peril.* ASHE-ERIC Higher Education Report No. 4. Washington, D.C.: The George Washington University, School of Education and Human Development.

Library of Congress Catalog Card Number 92-63194
ISSN 0884-0040
ISBN 1-878380-17-6

Managing Editor: Bryan Hollister
Manuscript Editor: Barbara Fishel, Editech
Cover design by Michael David Brown, Rockville, Maryland

The ERIC Clearinghouse on Higher Education invites individuals to submit proposals for writing monographs for the *ASHE-ERIC Higher Education Report* series. Proposals must include:
1. A detailed manuscript proposal of not more than five pages.
2. A chapter-by-chapter outline.
3. A 75-word summary to be used by several review committees for the initial screening and rating of each proposal.
4. A vita and a writing sample.

ERIC **Clearinghouse on Higher Education**
School of Education and Human Development
The George Washington University
One Dupont Circle, Suite 630
Washington, DC 20036-1183

This publication was prepared partially with funding from the Office of Educational Research and Improvement, U.S. Department of Education, under contract no. ED RI-88-062014. The opinions expressed in this report do not necessarily reflect the positions or policies of OERI or the Department.

EXECUTIVE SUMMARY

Until relatively recently, most research about job satisfaction was completed in the industrial sector, with attempts often made to adapt findings to higher education. Given the impending shortage of prospective faculty to fill the numerous vacancies that will exist by 2000, the topics of job satisfaction for faculty, recruitment, and retention must be given priority attention. Further, the faculty of the future must reflect the diversity of the population to be served by colleges and universities; consequently, immediate actions must be taken to ensure that the faculty position is attractive to women and minorities alike.

Who Will Fill Future Faculty Positions in Colleges and Universities?

Beginning in 2000 and continuing for several decades, a serious shortage will exist of persons to fill vacant faculty positions, with women and minorities clearly underrepresented in a variety of disciplines. Only a few minorities are now in the academic pipeline, and women and minorities who complete the doctorate often choose other occupations because they do not view the faculty position as a viable career choice. Clearly, salaries lag behind those offered by other professions, the faculty position does not command the revered status it once did, and many current faculty are dissatisfied with their choice of career. Unquestionably, such problems will dramatically affect the ability of colleges and universities to attract, nurture, develop, and retain women and minority faculty (Jones and Nowotny 1990). Consequently, institutional officials and current faculty in higher education must recognize the factors that lead to job dissatisfaction among faculty and eliminate them; conversely, they must recognize the factors that increase job satisfaction and enhance them.

What Are Some of the Stressors that Affect Women And Minority Faculty Members?

Internal stressors on faculty include achievement and recognition for achievement, autonomy, growth and development, the quality of students, the reputation of the institution and one's colleagues, responsibility, the interaction between students and teachers and its effect on students' learning, and the work itself. Factors in the workplace that prevent job dissatisfaction describe relationships to the context or environment in which individuals work, representing such variables as interpersonal relationships, salary, tenure, policies and administration, rank, supervision, working conditions, the "fit" between the faculty role and the person involved, and collective bargaining. Life-style stressors usually have a more dramatic effect on women than men because of societal norms about the priority women should place on their families. The list of life-style stressors is enormous but includes such items as child care, elder care, and physical as well as mental health; in addition, demands from the family and household, such as marriage and children, dual-career/ commuting marriages, and domestic responsibilities, dramatically affect the satisfaction and productivity of women faculty.

Are Women Disgruntled with Their Faculty Positions?
Women faculty members are less satisfied with their positions than their male counterparts. Today, women represent a small percentage of the faculty cohort, make lower salaries than their male colleagues, are found in the lower professorial ranks, are often employed in part-time rather than full-time positions, represent disciplines typically reserved for females, work in less prestigious institutions, feel that their supervisors do not value their input, and are not tenured.

It also appears that women enjoy and engage in teaching more often than research; interestingly, women must handle heavier teaching loads, a limitless number of student advisees, and more than their fair share of committee assignments while trying to carve out sufficient time for research and writing. In addition, women faculty have to prove themselves over and over again before they can be accepted by their colleagues and achieve recognition.

In addition to these issues, women are bombarded with life-style stressors that add unnecessary restrictions to their ability to achieve success in academe. In most instances, a woman faculty member gives up her own personal time to handle the demands associated with being a mother, wife, domestic servant, care giver for elderly parents, friend, colleague, author, invited speaker, researcher, teacher, committee member, and so on (Aisenberg and Harrington 1988). In effect, when a woman accepts a faculty position, she is really accepting a second or third job!

Clearly, if more women faculty are to be attracted to higher education and those who are currently employed are to remain, something must be done to enhance job satisfaction. Moreover, support services must be in place to help women balance the often conflicting demands of work and life. Unless changes are made in the way faculty work is completed, in the rewards associated with the professoriat, and in the way institutions help people deal with personal obstacles, women faculty could indeed become an endangered species in most disciplines.

The problem is more significant than simply bringing more women into the university. If we can solve the conflict between work and family, everyone will benefit and it is likely that more women will enter and stay in academe. The well-being of the university depends on its ability to recruit and retain a talented professorate. Our national well-being depends on our ability to develop a happy, emotionally healthy, and productive next generation (Hensel 1991, p. 79).

How Satisfied Are Minority Faculty with Their Faculty Positions?
When minority faculty are employed in institutions of higher education, some things are certain. When compared to their white counterparts, they are less likely to be tenured, are concentrated in the lower academic ranks, are often concerned about low salaries, feel isolated and unsupported at work, and often encounter prejudice, discrimination, and a continuing climate of racism. They are also often overburdened with student advising and counseling and institutional or community service. Unquestionably, these problems must be addressed if the number of minority faculty on college and university campuses is to increase (Silver, Dennis, and Spikes 1988).

Can Anything Be Done to Increase Job Satisfaction, Recruitment, and Retention of Women and Minority Faculty?
Leaders and faculty in higher education must implement a variety of recruiting and retention strategies if a faculty representing a diverse culture is to become a reality. Conventional (or traditional) approaches must be combined with fresh, extraordinary strategies, and long-term and short-term plans are necessary. Planning must begin with the enrollment of minorities into undergraduate and graduate programs in

decent numbers so they can eventually enter the pool for faculty positions; women must be attracted into disciplines where they are currently underrepresented. Institutions must include incentives for departments to diversify (for example, positions restricted to minority and women candidates, money to provide competitive salaries, and overt rewards for success). A variety of institutions have successfully used the following strategies (Green 1989; Justus, Freitag, and Parker 1987; Washington and Harvey 1989):

- Summer projects that provide an opportunity for underrepresented students to participate in faculty research projects;
- Guarantees of financial support (scholarships, assistantships, and fellowships) as well as guarantees of employment after completion of the doctorate to women and minorities who agree to enter the faculty;
- "Growing your own" minority and women faculty;
- The "two-for-one" approach, in which an additional position in a department or division is approved when a minority candidate is involved;
- Faculty exchange programs with historically black, Hispanic, and women's institutions;
- Research jobs or part-time teaching positions and post-doctoral fellowships;
- Employing women and minorities who have completed all requirements for the doctorate except the dissertation, with follow-up faculty development programs that permit them to complete their degrees while working as a faculty member;
- Exploration of untapped markets like business and industry and part-time faculty employees to reach individuals who might view the faculty position as a viable career option;
- Improved networking and opportunities for professional development, such as centers for minority and women faculty, research funds, early and honest communication about institutional and departmental standards for promotion and tenure, early sabbaticals, and release time for research; and
- General institutional support in the form of employment assistance for spouses or partners, salary differentials, and child care.

Clearly, the way colleges and universities recruit, retain, and reward women and minority faculty must radically and immediately change. Only then will the talents of women and minority faculty be unleashed, and only then will higher education be appropriately equipped to respond to the needs of a constantly changing society.

ADVISORY BOARD

CONSULTING EDITORS

Philip Altbach
State University of New York–Buffalo

A. Nancy Avakian
Metropolitan State University

Paula Y. Bagasao
University of California System

Margaret J. Barr
Texas Christian University

Barbara B. Burn
University of Massachusetts–Amherst

L. Edwin Coate
Oregon State University

Clifton F. Conrad
University of Wisconsin–Madison

Robert Cope
Northwoods Institute

John W. Creswell
University of Nebraska–Lincoln

Michael L. Hanes
West Chester University

Mary Ann Heverly
Delaware County Community College

Malcolm D. Hill
The Pennsylvania State University

Edward R. Hines
Illinois State University

Donald Hossler
Indiana University

Joan Isenberg
George Mason University

Donald Kirby
Le Moyne College

Richard D. Lambert
Johns Hopkins University

John B. Lee
JBL Associates

REVIEW PANEL

Charles Adams
University of Massachusetts–Amherst

Louis Albert
American Association for Higher Education

Richard Alfred
University of Michigan

Philip G. Altbach
State University of New York–Buffalo

Marilyn J. Amey
University of Kansas

Louis C. Attinasi, Jr.
University of Houston

Robert J. Barak
Iowa State Board of Regents

Alan Bayer
Virginia Polytechnic Institute and State University

John P. Bean
Indiana University

Louis W. Bender
Florida State University

John M. Braxton
Syracuse University

Peter McE. Buchanan
Council for Advancement and
    Support of Education

John A. Centra
Syracuse University

Arthur W. Chickering
George Mason University

Shirley M. Clark
Oregon State System of Higher Education

Darrel A. Clowes
Virginia Polytechnic Institute and State University

John W. Creswell
University of Nebraska–Lincoln

Deborah DiCroce
Piedmont Virginia Community College

Richard Duran
University of California

Kenneth C. Green
University of Southern California

Edward R. Hines
Illinois State University

Marsha W. Krotseng
West Virginia State College and University Systems

George D. Kuh
Indiana University–Bloomington

Daniel T. Layzell
Arizona Legislature

Meredith Ludwig
American Association of State Colleges and Universities

Mantha V. Mehallis
Florida Atlantic University

Robert J. Menges
Northwestern University

Toby Milton
Essex Community College

James R. Mingle
State Higher Education Executive Officers

Gary Rhoades
University of Arizona

G. Jeremiah Ryan
Harford Community College

Daryl G. Smith
Claremont Graduate School

William Tierney
Pennsylvania State University

Susan Twombly
University of Kansas

Harold Wechsler
University of Rochester

Michael J. Worth
George Washington University

CONTENTS

Foreword   **xvii**

Acknowledgments   **xix**

The Faculty in Higher Education: An Overview   **1**

Internal Stressors for Faculty   **9**

Work and Satisfaction   9

Teaching and Research   10

Reputation of Colleagues and the Institution   11

Quality of the Students   12

Interaction among Students and Teachers and

  Its Effect on Students' Learning   13

Autonomy and Responsibility   14

Achievement and Recognition for Achievement   15

Promotion and Growth   16

Summary   17

Factors in the Workplace Affecting Job Satisfaction   **19**

Salary   19

Tenure   22

Faculty Rank   24

Supervision   25

Interpersonal Relationships   26

Working Conditions   27

Policies and Administration   27

Person-Environment Fit   28

Collective Bargaining   29

Summary   31

Women Faculty   **33**

Job Satisfaction, Women, and the Workplace   34

Internal Stressors   35

Factors in the Workplace   38

Life-style Stressors   42

Summary   52

Minority Faculty   **55**

The Need for and Status of Minority Faculty   55

Attitudes and Perceptions of Minority Faculty

  About Job Satisfaction   58

Overall Job Satisfaction   59

Summary   73

**Issues and Strategies for Recruiting and
Retaining Women and Minority Faculty**   **75**

Addressing the Problem of the Pipeline   76

Making the Faculty Position an Attractive and
  Viable Career Option 83
Providing General Institutional Support 89
Providing Incentives to Diversify the Faculty 92
Summary 96

References **99**
Index **115**

FOREWORD

Research on why people enjoy their work has identified four major areas that produce satisfaction. First and most important is that people feel appreciated for their efforts. Second is their perception that their efforts have a significant impact. Third is working or living in an environmentally pleasing or aesthetic location. And fourth is the equity in the remuneration for their work. The degree that a person is satisfied with each area is quite idiosyncratic. What does not vary is an individual's need to have an overall sense of well-being when all four areas are taken as a whole. This sense of satisfaction is especially critical for higher education for two reasons: quality of work and developing future faculty.

Most satisfied workers perform at their maximum capacity for the good of the organization; most dissatisfied workers seek to increase their satisfaction by working for their own advantage. In a highly structured and supervised work area, either condition could only slightly affect the quality of performance. But in higher education, where faculty have considerable discretion over how they spend their time, job dissatisfaction can result in an enormous decrease in quality. For example, the normative behavior dictated by the concept of academic freedom can result in a very positive sense of professionalism in some and a feeling of abandonment and lack of appreciation in others. The balance between allowing freedom to create knowledge and providing enough attention to provide appreciation takes conscious effort if it is to be effective.

Satisfaction for faculty is also very important in influencing the quality of future faculty. Using the system approach exemplified in Peter Senge's *The Fifth Discipline: The Art and Practice of the Learning Organization* (New York: Doubleday, 1990), this influence can be displayed as follows:

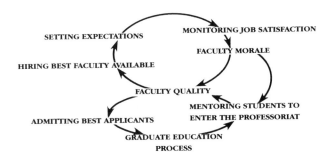

The quality of faculty is determined initially by the quality of people hired. Their performance is then influenced by articulated expectations and by what is observed as the patterns of success. As the faculty member continues to work, the fluctuating feeling of satisfaction and dissatisfaction influences morale and the quality of faculty's work. Interconnected with this process are the graduate schools, which first determine their standards by the ability of the faculty to attract quality students. Through experience in graduate education, these students then develop expectations about their future careers. If faculty who experience high job satisfaction are their mentors, they are then more likely to choose the academic profession as a career. If faculty morale is low, then students are likely to choose another area for a career.

Consideration of factors that influence job satisfaction is important not only for the overall quality of the faculty, but also in consideration of distinctive faculty groups, such as women and minorities. If higher education is serious about attracting and retaining women and minorities in the faculty, then what creates satisfaction or dissatisfaction for these individuals must be specifically considered.

Martha Wingard Tack, professor and head of the Department of Leadership and Counseling at Eastern Michigan University, and Carol Logan Patitu, executive assistant to the vice president for student affairs at Miami University (Ohio) first examine the concepts of faculty job satisfaction and then look specifically at issues and strategies that relate to recruiting and retaining women and minority faculty.

Developing and maintaining a high-quality faculty does not happen by accident. It takes leadership sensitive to the issues that help to create optimal working conditions. Higher education can no longer afford the employment practice of benign neglect so often used on faculty, who are primarily tenured full professors. Knowing what conditions influence job satisfaction for faculty generally and for women and minorities specifically will contribute significantly to developing a faculty of excellence.

Jonathan D. Fife
Series Editor, Professor of Higher Education
Administration, and Director, ERIC
Clearinghouse on Higher Education,
The George Washington University

ACKNOWLEDGMENTS

As this report documents, when women are involved in dual-career marriages, have children, and devote time to scholarship, they must have exceptionally strong support systems in place if they are to be successful. The authors have such support systems and wish to acknowledge the important people in their lives who have been there so they could complete their work.

In the Tack household, Jason and Jarrod, Martha's teenage sons, have eaten fast food nearly daily, greeted her cheerfully when she was "late again" for dinner, and finally stopped asking why she had to work on weekends. Gary Heberlein, Martha's husband, made significant sacrifices of his personal and professional time throughout the long process of writing this manuscript. He basically assumed sole responsibility for the family during this time, even though he also had to handle an exceptionally demanding position as vice president for research and dean of the Graduate School at Wayne State University. To them, Martha sends a huge "thank you" and a big "I love you!"

Carol's husband, Tony, offered unending support as she devoted every waking moment when she was not in the office to reading and writing. As Carol hurried to finish her work before the birth of their first child, Tony took care of everything else. To him and to their new son, Tony, Carol extends her unending love and devotion. In addition, Carol wishes to acknowledge her parents, Joseph and Julia Logan, and other family members who never complained about the canceled weekend visits to Marion, Ohio, for special family occasions so she could devote time to this project.

In addition to family members, numerous friends and colleagues also offered assistance and moral support that helped Carol and Martha persevere. To the people at Eastern Michigan University who worked overtime to help her meet deadlines, Martha is especially grateful; thanks specifically go to Jacqueline Simon for her expertise and dedication to excellence as she searched library resources for materials that might be useful and for spending several sleepless nights working on the manuscript so it could be mailed on time. Barbara Eupizi and Lisa Hilton also provided tremendous help in completing ERIC searches and locating books. At Miami University, Carol extends her gratitude to Sandy Williams for her willingness to help and her hard work in locating materials for review. Carol and Martha also want to acknowledge Beth Sweitzer, a steadfast friend, for her constant reinforcement, support, and caring. Finally, Carol and Martha express sincere appreciation to Dr. Jonathan Fife for providing encouragement and demonstrating his confidence in their ability to get the job done. Without these people, this report never would have become a reality.

This manuscript is dedicated to two very special people in Martha's and Carol's lives, their mothers—the late Leota Stokes Wingard and Julia Elizabeth Logan—for their love, their sage advice, and their high aspirations for what women can truly accomplish.

THE FACULTY IN HIGHER EDUCATION: An Overview

In the next two decades, the composition and availability of faculty for higher education institutions will change dramatically, changes that portend significant challenges for the academy. Severe shortages of qualified faculty in nearly all disciplines (with a shortage of crisis proportions for minority and women faculty) will mandate improved working conditions as a means of enhancing job satisfaction, an upgraded image of the faculty position, and an increase in the value of compensation packages. In addition, unnecessarily complex "life-style stressors" that faculty must deal with should be eliminated to encourage minorities and women to pursue a career in the professoriat. Higher education officials will soon have to deal with some significant changes:

"Compared to other occupations chosen by college graduates, university and college teaching is slightly less attractive than it was in the early 1970s."

1. *The supply of instructional personnel from which to select the thousands of new full-time faculty members required in the future will be inadequate.* The scenario for the future seems bleak (American Association of University 1992): "Compared to other occupations chosen by college graduates, university and college teaching is slightly less attractive than it was in the early 1970s" (p. 9), and "American attitudes toward higher education seem so negative today that still more of the retirees of the 1990s will not be replaced—and those who continue teaching will not see the boom in salaries that they might have expected" (p. 9). Nearly 340,000 faculty members have to be hired to replace those who will retire by 2004, making "the marketplace of academe, relatively stagnant for nearly two decades, . . . destined to vibrate with activity" (Schuster 1990, p. 35). In California alone, it is anticipated that by 2000 nearly two-thirds of the current faculty in public postsecondary institutions (approximately 24,000 positions) will need to be replaced because of retirement.

In addition to the problems associated with the faculty in general, a major dilemma will exist in terms of locating and hiring qualified minorities and women faculty members, individuals who are essential to higher education, especially if it is to reflect and respond to the society it serves. It is clear that "while some progress has been made, a truly heterogeneous faculty has not yet been realized" (Jacobs 1990, p. 47).

Minority groups constitute about 20 to 25 percent of the U.S. population, but they occupy only 8 to 10 percent of the faculty positions in higher education (Bowen and Schuster 1986). Even this percentage is somewhat skewed because of the heavy participation of Asians, who represented 21,000 of the 489,000 full-time, regular instructional faculty in institutions of higher education (or 4.3 percent of the faculty cohort) during academic year 1987–88 (U.S. Dept. of Education 1991). "Nonwhite women were represented by the same number in 1984 as in 1975 (7 percent), and the percentage of nonwhite men went from 5.7 percent in 1974 to 7 percent in 1984" (Jacobs 1990, p. 47). In addition, the presence of Native American and Hispanic faculty is minimal at best, even in geographical areas where they account for a major portion of the population. Clearly, improvement is required if the academy is to create an ethnically diverse faculty.

"Women, who constituted 22.3 percent of full-time instructional faculty in 1972–73, constituted only 23 percent in 1985–86, after 15 years of concerted effort to increase the proportion of female faculty members" (Jacobs 1990, p. 47). Moreover, these women are typically clustered in traditionally feminine disciplines and in nontenured instructor/assistant professor positions, and they are employed primarily at two-year colleges.

The problems of representation by minorities on faculties in postsecondary institutions are further exacerbated by the facts that only a few minorities are currently in the educational pipeline and that it takes approximately 10.5 years from receipt of a baccalaureate to complete a doctorate. "There is virtually no way that adequate numbers of suitably qualified prospective faculty members will be available [before the end of the 1990s]" (Schuster 1990, p. 37). Unquestionably, the competition for the few minorities who hold terminal degrees will be fierce in all fields, including business and industry, and it is likely that institutional and corporate raiding will become an accepted way of doing business as all colleges and universities feel the mounting pressure to hire role models for minority students.

2. *Faculty salaries will become even more central in attracting young men and women into the professoriat and will without a doubt significantly affect their job satisfaction.* "The most satisfied faculty members are paid about $6,000 more than the average . . . and earn at least $2,800 more than the median salary for all faculty members" (Carnegie Foundation 1986, pp. 32–33).

Most people enter the faculty ranks for reasons other than economic ones.

To faculty members, the intrinsic rewards of academic life—not salaries—have always been the most important issue. But faculty members do not view compensation as unimportant. And compensation for the professoriate, expressed in terms of real earnings adjusted for inflation, has dropped sharply—by about 15 percent since 1970 (Schuster 1986, p. 278).

Average academic-year salaries for full-time faculty increased significantly from 1965–66 ($9,816) to 1987–88 ($37,000) (Andersen, Carter, and Malizio 1989), but faculty salaries continue to lag behind salaries in other sectors of society like business and industry. The decline in real income also poses another issue, as "the cumulative loss in real earnings for faculty since the early 1970s appears to be greater than that for any other major, nonagricultural occupation" (Schuster 1990, p. 34). Unfortunately:

Between academic years 1990–91 and 1991–92, the average salary of faculty in the United States rose by 3.5 percent . . . the smallest nominal increase in over 20 years. . . . The two-year period 1989–90 to 1991–92 showed the slowest real growth in academic salaries since the early 1980s (American Association of University 1992, p. 7).

3. *During the past four years, several national studies on college and university faculty have tended to describe the faculty as a group who, "despite stress and demoralization, have managed on the whole to remain committed, dedicated, resourceful, and resilient"* (Schuster 1986, p. 282; see also Bowen and Schuster 1986; Carnegie Foundation 1989; U.S. Dept. of Education 1990). In fact, an analysis of faculty perceptions revealed "an overall positive attitude about the profession itself" (Carnegie Foundation 1989, p. 69), and 86 percent of the faculty in one survey reported they were "very" or at least "somewhat" satisfied with their job overall (U.S. Dept. of Education 1990).

Like so many other topics in postsecondary education, conflicting opinions exist about the status and morale of the faculty in higher education. Based on the evidence available, however, it is probably safe to say that, even though the situation has improved somewhat over the past few years, "the status of faculty members has declined" (Schuster 1990, p. 34) and "faculty morale is low, a condition exacerbated by rapidly shifting values that are contributing to discord and frustration on many campuses" (Schuster 1986, pp. 277–78).

Regardless of positive indicators about the profession itself, based on information collected by the National Center for Education Statistics (NCES) in cooperation with SRI International and the Center for the Study of Higher Education at Pennsylvania State University, "sizable portions of faculty members indicated that they would consider leaving their institutions, and higher education altogether, if the right opportunity appeared . . . [, revealing] an undercurrent of dissatisfaction with prevailing conditions in academe" (Schuster 1990, p. 37). Thirty-one percent of the individuals involved in one survey indicated that they might leave the profession within the next five years, a disturbing thought when coupled with the predicted shortages of qualified new faculty (Carnegie Foundation 1989). In addition, while about three-fourths of the faculty disagreed with the statement, "I often wish I had entered another profession," slightly more than one-fourth of the respondents were not so optimistic; moreover, 15 percent said, "I would not become a college teacher if I had it to do over again." Many faculty are dissatisfied with their positions for a variety of reasons: poor working conditions, a perception that their workload has increased over the years, demands to publish or perish, lack of rewards, and geographic immobility, among others.

Furthermore, "college administrators have tended to underestimate the divisiveness and bitterness that the shifting values on campuses have engendered" (Schuster 1986, p. 281). For example, values have shifted from undergraduate to graduate teaching, and greater value is often associated with research and scholarship than with teaching or service. The perceived diminution of the faculty role in governance over several years "is in some cases a source of resigned disappointment, in others a cause of serious faculty discontent, and in all a source of poor morale" (Bowen and Schuster 1986, p. 128). "As a consequence . . . , faculty morale, by most accounts, has been uneven, dropping to very low levels on many campuses" (Schuster 1990, p. 34).

4. *University officials will be called upon to provide both personal attention to and professional development for two diverse age groups of faculty: a large group of young and inexperienced junior faculty members and a significant cadre of senior faculty approaching retirement age.* Given that the needs of these two groups of faculty differ significantly, support systems and training programs will have to be developed that respond creatively to the issues associated with dramatic differences in age, maturity, and employment experience. Moreover, the removal of a mandatory retirement age and the existence of tenure as a component of job security support the indefinite involvement in college and university life of senior faculty, whose overall compensation packages are costly.

Certainly, college and university officials must consider the role that job satisfaction plays in the ability of an institution to attract, nurture, develop, and retain a top-quality faculty that is diverse in gender, race, age, socioeconomic level, and so on. When people are disenchanted with their work, high absenteeism and low productivity usually result. Unquestionably, then, it is time to look at the work the faculty perform and the environment in which the work is completed, with an eye toward identifying the factors that enhance satisfaction and eliminating the stimuli that create dissatisfaction. University and college officials must deal with issues that create job dissatisfaction as a means of retaining minority and women faculty who have become discontent with their positions. Moreover, intense efforts must be made to recruit talented individuals who otherwise would not be attracted to faculty positions.

While the research literature is relatively silent when it comes to faculty job satisfaction, existing "to the point of paucity" (Winkler 1982, p. 16), a wealth of information exists on the topic of job satisfaction in general, with most of the research having been completed in the U.S. industrial sector. For example, 2,174 articles on job satisfaction were indexed in the Educational Resources Information Center (ERIC) and 3,020 in the Psycinfo systems from 1970 to July 1992 (another 4,000 had been written before then [Locke 1969]). While it is possible that some articles were listed in both ERIC and Psycinfo, it is clear that the topic is of interest to researchers and writers alike. In addition to these articles, 4,096 other documents on job satisfaction (papers presented at meetings, evaluative reports, and course syllabi as well as other instructional materials) were prepared during this 22-year time frame. Of the 5,194 articles in the ERIC and Psycinfo systems published between 1970 and July 1992, however, only 300 were related to job satisfaction of faculty in higher education, and only 414 of the other documents on job satisfaction developed during the same 22-year period were related to faculty job satisfaction. "Perhaps this area has not received attention because a high level of job satisfaction generally has been presumed to exist in a university setting" (Pearson and Seiler 1983, p. 36). "Current conditions, however, indicate that the time for a closer look at this aspect of academic life may be in order" (p. 46).

To understand the concept of job satisfaction as it relates to college and university professors, an elementary understanding of job satisfaction theory must exist. In that regard, "no single theory seems to give a satisfactory explanation" of job satisfaction (Ben-Porat 1981, p. 532), but traditional views on the topic indicate that satisfaction and dissatisfaction are simple opposites. In contrast, the most widely cited and accepted theory for explaining job satisfaction in the industrial sector is Herzberg's theory of job satisfaction (Herzberg 1966).[1] Regardless:

> *Most professors regard their work not as a job that can be separated from their other responsibilities and interests but rather as a central thread woven through all aspects of their lives, blurring the boundary between the personal and the professional* (Austin and Pilat 1990, p. 38).

Nevertheless, personnel in higher education must be aware of the factors leading to job dissatisfaction among faculty and then try to eliminate them, as well as enhance the factors that motivate faculty to work at peak levels of effectiveness and efficiency. "In the long run, nothing is more central to the quality of higher education than working conditions that make teaching and research on our campuses a more satisfying

---

1. This theory, known more formally as the Motivator-Hygiene Theory, Herzberg's Two-Factor Theory, or the Two-Factor or Dual-Factor Theory of Job Satisfaction, is discussed fully in Herzberg 1966, Herzberg et al. 1957, and Herzberg, Mausner, and Snyderman 1959.

career" (Carnegie Foundation 1986, p. 34). Therefore, leaders in higher education must be willing to provide working conditions that are satisfying as well as competitive with those in other professions (Bowen and Schuster 1986). Clearly, recruitment and retention of and job satisfaction among faculty in higher education must become a national priority if a qualified faculty, representative of women and minorities, is to exist in the future.

INTERNAL STRESSORS FOR FACULTY

Internal stressors contributing directly to faculty members' job satisfaction include teaching and research, the reputation of colleagues and the institution, the quality of the students, interaction among students and teachers and its effect on students' learning, autonomy and responsibility, achievement and recognition for achievement, and promotion and growth. Clearly, these internal stressors contribute to job satisfaction among faculty and to the decision to remain with or leave an institution of higher education altogether. Before reviewing the literature on these seven internal stressors, it is necessary to understand the concept of faculty job satisfaction.

Work and Satisfaction

Work is one of the most absorbing things men can think and talk about. It fills the greater part of the waking day for most of us. For the fortunate it is the source of great satisfactions; for many others it is the cause of grief (Herzberg, Mausner, and Snyderman 1959, p. 3).

Moreover, work can be perceived as fascinating, satisfying, creative, or repetitive. More than 25 years ago, it was found that the strongest influence on job choice for most professors was the "opportunity for meaningful professional activity" (Brown 1967, p. 151). The seven factors related to meaningful activities for faculty include courses taught, teaching load, research facilities and opportunities, competency of colleagues, reputation of the school, quality of students, and the nature of administration and administrators (Brown 1967).

Other researchers have described other attributes related to interest in one's work and satisfaction derived from it:

- The opportunity to use valued skills and abilities (Alderfer 1967)
- A chance to learn (Patchen 1970)
- Room to be creative (Lawler and Hall 1970)
- Greater control (Lawler and Hall 1970)
- Job enrichment (Maher 1971)
- Responsibility (Locke 1973)
- Difficulty of the work (Patchen 1970).

"In the absence of an adequate mental challenge or in the presence of a . . . task that is accomplished automatically (with no effort, skill, or thought required), one experiences *boredom,* which is the converse of interest" (Locke 1976, pp. 1319–20). Consequently, an intellectual challenge could be of utmost importance to faculty in higher education.

> *Strongly held, too, were the positive possibilities in their work for the realization of personal satisfactions and growth and opportunities for intellectual stimulation. The exercise and use of the mind and an environment for the development of the whole person, mind and body, were key elements of the satisfaction of faculty* (Diener 1984, p. 12).

Further, "there is some evidence that younger workers place greater weight than do older ones on intrinsic job factors, such as degree of challenge, diversity, and freedom" (Katzell 1979, p. 40). Yet if the challenge is too great for the person, the job can then become a source of frustration (Locke 1976).

Teaching and Research
Teaching and research are two of the most important activities performed by faculty. Some believe that the faculty's major satisfactions are received from the work itself (i.e., teaching, research, and service) (Diener 1984). When faculty were asked "From where do you derive the most satisfaction on your current position? . . . In other words, what do you like best about your job here?" (Wissman 1981, p. 58), teaching was reported as the most satisfying responsibility.

For courses taught, professors prefer attractive teaching assignments. They might ask what the subject of the course is, whether they are attracted to it, how many students can enroll in the class, and how many classes they will be teaching. A research-oriented professor would not want to be so overwhelmed with teaching that he or she has no time for research. Interestingly, "faculty at doctoral-degree-granting institutions perceive their departments value research ($x = 4.28$) much higher than teaching ($x = 3.48$)" (Steen, Giunipero, and Newgren 1985, p. 352), although older faculty members usually enjoy teaching more than their younger counterparts (see, e.g., Murray 1983).

Research, not teaching, however, is valued more today than in the past, especially by individuals who make decisions involving personnel. Although faculty at the University of Texas at Arlington, for example, ranked teaching as the most important criterion of ideal performance, research and publication were thought to be the highest priority in decisions affecting personnel (Hunter, Ventimiglia, and Crow 1980). Other criteria besides publication, research, and teaching included school service, public service, student advising, and seniority. Furthermore, "publications have become the primary measure of scholarship, easily superseding teaching as the criterion for professional success" (Newell and Spear 1983, p. 110).

Researchers found that 54 percent of more than 5,000 faculty from all types of higher education institutions agreed that, in their department, it is difficult for a person to achieve tenure if he or she does not publish (Carnegie Foundation 1989). For faculty at four-year institutions, the percentage was higher—77 percent. The percentage differed, depending on the Carnegie classification of the institution: for faculty at research institutions, 94 percent; for faculty at doctoral-degree-granting institutions, 89 percent; for faculty at comprehensive institutions, 65 percent; for faculty at liberal arts institutions, 39 percent; and for faculty at two-year institutions, 6 percent. Even though faculty prefer to teach, they spend a substantial amount of time conducting research, whether or not it is to enhance opportunities for promotion. For instance, full-time faculty work an average of 62 hours each week, with approximately 23 of those hours devoted to research or creative activities (Institute for Research 1978). Further, during the 62-hour work week, faculty spend about 27 hours on teaching, 7.5 hours on university service, and about five hours on activities associated with their professions or public service.

Opportunities for research might not always be available, however. For example, 33 percent of the faculty in one study viewed opportunities for research as "quite a problem" or "a major problem" (Diener 1984). Nevertheless, "pressure in academic institutions is mounting steadily in the direction of performance in research and scholarly writing as requisites for faculty advancement and security, i.e., promotion and tenure" (Murray 1983, p. 88).

Reputation of Colleagues and the Institution
The competence of colleagues is an important factor in job satisfaction, because the reputation of individual professors is affected by the reputation of the department in which they work. In addition, the prestige of the institution or its rep-

". . . the reputation of individual professors is affected by the reputation of the department in which they work."

utation is an especially critical variable for "young men [or young women] on the way up, for they cherish a stimulating, research-publication atmosphere where they may draw upon the talents of established scholars to build their own reputations" (Brown 1967, p. 156).

In one study, 87.1 percent (196) of the faculty were either "somewhat satisfied," "satisfied," or "very satisfied" with the reputation of their school; only 16 respondents (7.3 percent) indicated that they were dissatisfied at some level (Cavenar 1987). The mean degree of satisfaction with the reputation of the school was 5.9 on a scale of one to seven, with one being "very dissatisfied" and seven being "very satisfied."

Quality of the Students
The quality of students is very important to some faculty members. In fact, the pervasive finding in one study was strong faculty concern for quality, not only in their colleagues and in their work environment but also in their students (Boberg and Blackburn 1983).

In interviews, some members of the arts faculty in an Australian university "spoke of some of the consequences of maintaining numbers by admitting a larger number of less able students. These consequences included more remedial teaching and less contact with good students" (Powell, Barrett, and Shanker 1983, p. 301). In fact, some faculty might enjoy teaching only "good," "able," or "quality" students.

In talking about the nature of the satisfaction to be gained from teaching, some [faculty] spoke of the pleasure of seeing students gain in understanding and of working with very able students who are able to stimulate the teacher's own thinking (Powell, Barrett, and Shanker 1983, p. 300).

Another reason faculty might be dissatisfied with "poor" students is that they "take more time away from other faculty pursuits, especially at comprehensive universities where faculty are under greater pressure to publish more and still have to deal with less qualified students" (Boberg and Blackburn 1983, p. 10). Furthermore, 68 percent of all faculty in one study agreed that their institution spends too much time and money teaching students what they should have learned in high school (Carnegie Foundation 1989).

Interaction among Students and Teachers
And its Effect on Students' Learning

"Interaction with students should be the chief intrinsic motivation" for faculty (Cohen 1974, p. 373). A study of 222 community college instructors from 12 institutions found that "more than two-thirds of the group indicated that they gained satisfaction from student learning or from interaction with students . . . " (Cohen 1974, p. 369). Faculty-student interaction is important for faculty members; "faculty who have more contact with students also are more likely to be 'very satisfied' with the stimulation they receive from students" (Wilson, Woods, and Gaff 1974, p. 88). "Seeing and supporting student growth was by far the chief source of [the faculty's] satisfaction. Almost eight of ten faculty declared interaction with students and having the opportunity to have some impact on their lives is their principal joy" (Diener 1984, p. 12).

In a study of teacher educators, only four items on the "Professional Satisfaction Scale," one of three instruments used in the research, exceeded four on a scale of one to five, with five being "highly satisfied." "Working with Students" led with a score of 4.484; therefore, "it appears that teacher educators derive a great deal of satisfaction in working with students . . . " (Nussel, Wiersma, and Rusche 1988, p. 50). In another study, faculty reported working with students as the second most popular response to the question "From where do you derive the most satisfaction in your current position?" (Wissman 1981, p. 58). Of the 98 responses by 80 subjects, 16 (16.3 percent) dealt with "Working with Students." (The number of responses [98] is greater than the number of subjects [80], because some people gave two responses.)

More recently, researchers found that 83 percent of all faculty agreed they enjoy interacting informally with undergraduates outside the classroom (Carnegie Foundation 1989). For faculty at four-year and two-year institutions, the percentages were 83 percent and 84 percent, respectively. Based on Carnegie classifications, the percentages were as follows: research institutions, 77 percent; doctoral-degree-granting institutions, 83 percent; comprehensive colleges and universities, 85 percent; liberal arts colleges, 92 percent; and two-year institutions, 84 percent. "The extent of instructor-student interaction is related to faculty members' belief that it is an important part of the educational process" (Yuker 1984, pp. 53–54).

Autonomy and Responsibility

Faculty typically expect autonomy and academic freedom and are therefore concerned about administrative intervention or infringement in these areas. In one study, freedom and independence in work were highly rated aspects of working conditions (Diener 1984). Another study notes that high autonomy of thought and action in areas of expertise was a clear motivator to participants (Toombs and Marlier 1981). In that study, the 134 interviewees had left Pennsylvania State University during calendar years 1978 and 1979. Participants in the study who transferred to other academic situations (57) were asked about sources of satisfaction in their new situation; ". . . 'autonomy' and 'improved collegial relations' . . . brought new satisfaction" (p. 28). In another survey, 87.6 percent of the part-time faculty respondents and 89.2 percent of the full-time faculty respondents from one community college were either "very satisfied" or "satisfied" with opportunities "to work alone on the job" (Neely 1981, p. 53). Further, on most campuses faculty members were satisfied that their autonomy had been "reasonably well preserved" (Bowen and Schuster 1986, p. 144).

"Many people enjoy the mental challenge that autonomy and responsibility provide because it gives them a chance to grow" (Locke, Fitzpatrick, and White 1983, p. 345). The majority of the 267 part-time respondents and the 157 full-time respondents in one study were satisfied with their responsibilities as measured by responses to the statement, "The freedom to use my own judgment," on the Minnesota Satisfaction Questionnaire (Neely 1981). Interestingly, 94 percent of the part-time faculty and 84 percent of the full-time faculty selected "satisfied" or "very satisfied" for their response.

For academics . . . their prestigious and autonomous work enables them, to a much larger extent than is possible for the general population, to fulfill both higher-order needs, i.e., esteem needs and needs for self-actualization. . . . Autonomy is such that each academic is largely responsible for the courses he/she teaches and for the research carried out. In addition, the timetabling of all the different activities is influenced by his/her preferences (Moses 1986, pp. 136–37).

Autonomy is declining, however, particularly in teaching. Several factors are perceived as limiting academics' traditional autonomy: course committees, reviews, accreditation procedures, evaluation, and general accountability measures (Moses 1986). Further, "external/financial constraints on faculty remuneration and accountability demands that increase 'red tape' and decrease autonomy probably contribute to continuing declines in faculty job satisfaction ratings" (Plascak-Craig and Bean 1989, p. 2). Twenty-seven percent of the faculty in one study viewed red tape (bureaucratic rules and excessive paperwork) as "quite a problem" or "a major problem" (Diener 1984).

Achievement and Recognition for Achievement

Achievement and recognition for achievement can also be internal stressors related to job satisfaction. One definition of achievement includes its opposite, failure, as well as the absence of achievement (Herzberg, Mausner, and Snyderman 1959). Specifically mentioned successes included "successful completion of a job, solutions to problems, vindication, and seeing the results of one's work" (p. 45). Recognition for achievement can come from a faculty member's chair, colleague, secretary, student, and administrator or from the university as a whole.

Virtually all employees value being praised for their work and being given credit where credit is due, especially by supervisors and colleagues whose judgment they respect. Similarly, most employees disvalue being criticized or not getting credit for their work accomplishments (Locke 1976, p. 1324).

In a study of postsecondary education faculty members employed in state-supported schools in Idaho, respondents were asked to identify factors that contributed to their feeling exceptionally good about their jobs (Hilton 1985). Of the 56 respondents from Idaho's public two-year postsecondary vocational education institutions (North Idaho College, Eastern Idaho Vocational Technical, and the College of Southern Idaho), 28 (50 percent) identified "recognition" as a very important factor. In the same study, of the 132 respondents from Idaho's public four-year postsecondary vocational education institutions (Boise State University, Idaho State Uni-

versity, and Lewis-Clark State College), 71 (54 percent) identified "recognition" as a factor that contributed to their feeling exceptionally good about their jobs.

A study of college professors showed that "college professors . . . are basically satisfied with their jobs when their efforts are recognized by someone, when they feel they have accomplished something, and when their jobs are interesting and challenging" (Leon 1973, p. 103). Thus, the main satisfiers were "recognition," "achievement," and "the work itself" (Leon 1973). Further, recent college graduates tend to be more concerned with personal "recognition" and responsibility than older workers, who tend to be more concerned with prestigious titles and money (Bass and Barrett 1975).

> *In this respect there is much that college administrators can do to improve the satisfying aspects of the college teaching job, especially in the area of recognition. For instance, most deans and department chairmen frequently receive reports from students on the good performance of professors [that], if passed on to the individual, would reinforce good performance and have a positive effect on the satisfaction of the professor and the continuation of such good performance. It is a basic aspect of the learning process that human beings have a need to know how well they are doing and that when they receive feedback that confirms and recognizes good performance, behavior is reinforced* (Leon 1973, p. 96).

Promotion and Growth

Promotion can be thought of as the affirmation of self-worth and as a reward for work well done. "Satisfaction with promotions can be viewed . . . as a function of the frequency of promotion in relation to what is desired and the importance of promotion to the individual" (Locke 1976, p. 1323). On the one hand:

> *It is easily conceivable that an employee could appraise the promotion system in his company as fair, and yet still be dissatisfied with his chances for promotion simply because there were none. Such an individual's value standard would depend upon his personal ambitions and career aspirations* (Locke 1976, p. 1323).

On the other hand, while most employees could view the promotion process where they work as being unfair, some employees could still be personally satisfied with the system. In effect, these people might have no desire to be promoted because they do not want the increased responsibility or more difficult work (Locke 1976).

Most professors look forward to being promoted through the ranks, from assistant professor to associate professor to full professor. Some faculty, however, are dissatisfied with opportunities for promotion. In a study of faculty in a southeastern state, 27 percent viewed opportunities for promotion as "quite a problem" or "a major problem" (Diener 1984).

Summary

Numerous internal stressors (for example, the work itself, teaching and research, the reputation of colleagues and the institution, the quality of students, interaction among students and teachers and its effect on students' learning, autonomy and responsibility, achievement and recognition for achievement, and growth and promotion) can affect the level of job satisfaction of faculty in higher education. Because teaching and research are two of the most important activities faculty perform, lack of satisfaction with these activities could certainly cause one to leave the profession. The competence of colleagues is also an important factor in job satisfaction because faculty members do not want their records tarnished from a bad reputation of their colleagues or institution. Like reputation, the quality of students is very important to most faculty. And many faculty consider interaction with students and students' learning as chief sources of satisfaction.

Autonomy and responsibility are also critical factors in faculty job satisfaction; in fact, some people have chosen to become faculty members because of the autonomy and responsibility the profession has to offer. As noted, however, the autonomy associated with being a faculty member is declining, particularly in terms of teaching (Moses 1986).

Most faculty members work hard to achieve goals and want to be recognized for their efforts through such avenues as promotion, tenure, and professional development. Most professors look forward to being promoted, and, if they are not promoted, they usually are not satisfied with their work.

Unquestionably, lack of satisfaction with internal stressors can cause faculty members to become discouraged; in many cases, disgruntled faculty look elsewhere for a suitable working environment. Given this information, institutional officials must concentrate their attention on providing an environment conducive to satisfaction for faculty members.

FACTORS IN THE WORKPLACE AFFECTING JOB SATISFACTION

Certain factors in the workplace (i.e., the collegiate environment and the conditions under which a faculty member must work) contribute directly to an institution's ability to recruit and retain women and minority faculty. Moreover, such factors significantly affect a faculty member's satisfaction or dissatisfaction with his or her professorial work. Therefore, higher education institutions must consider carefully the impact of several factors on women and minority faculty: salary, tenure (faculty job security), faculty rank, supervision, interpersonal relationships, working conditions, policies and administration, the person-environment fit, and collective bargaining. If college and university officials and board members do not address the factors that create dissatisfaction among women and minority faculty, women and minorities will seek satisfaction elsewhere—at other institutions, in other occupations, or in other types of organizations.

Salary

The degree to which salary affects job satisfaction is debatable.

> *No doubt, some workers are motivated solely by money and look at the world of work as a market place where they can exchange their time for money. There are other workers, however, who wish to be active in their jobs and express themselves through the medium of work* (Sheppard and Herrick 1972, p. 10).

While the relationship between salary and job satisfaction is debatable, salary also appears to be one of the greatest sources of *dissatisfaction* (Edmundson 1969; Ladd 1979; Winkler 1982).

"For academics generally, tenured and well-paid employment provides satisfaction of the lower-order needs" (Moses 1986, p. 136), such as physiological needs, safety, and security. A certain level of pay will keep faculty from being dissatisfied (Sprague 1974). Salary and fringe benefits, certain administrative features (e.g., involvement in such things as decisions about faculty hiring and termination and about campus promotion and tenure, general policy making, and extracurricular activities), and collegial associations should emerge as principal contributors to job satisfaction or dissatisfaction for college faculty (Hill 1987). Further, the "perceived inequities in wages and salaries tend to contribute more to [workers'] dissatisfaction than the exact amount of pay" (Ivancevich and Donnelly 1968, p. 176). Certainly, pay for performance could affect an individual's level of job satisfaction.

Furthermore, individuals might exert less effort to reduce the inequity if they believe they are being underpaid (Stoner 1982). In this case, they might experience dissatisfaction and be more likely to have feelings of anger and resentment (Patchen 1961). "Overpaid workers, on the other hand (also in a state of tension through perceived inequity), may work harder" (Stoner 1982, p. 463), and they are likely to experience feelings of guilt (Harrison 1979). Clearly, lower job satisfaction or dissatisfaction leads to certain kinds of behavior to rectify the inequity (Sprague 1974).

The reduction of inequity occurs "(1) by actually altering either inputs or outcomes, (2) by perceptually distorting inputs or outcomes, (3) by leaving the field, (4) by getting the comparison person to change, or (5) by changing to another comparison person" (Weick 1966, p. 418). As stated earlier, people can cognitively distort their perceived input-output ratios to reduce perceived inequity. For instance, some individuals might use their socioeconomic, educational, and cultural backgrounds to modify their and/or others' input-output ratios (Chung 1977), thus reducing a perceived inequity. For example, a white male with an Ivy League education might feel that his salary should be higher than a female worker with a college education (Chung 1977). He might feel the same way toward an African-American or other minority male or female, even if that person is a better performer than he is. A cognitive distortion of this nature has a limitation, however, because it can create feelings of self-deception and guilt (Chung 1977). "Leaving the field or retreating from the exchange relationship is viewed as a last resort, occurring only when inequity is great and other means of reducing it seem to be unavailable" (Campbell and Pritchard 1976, p. 105). Thus, in spite of the amount of pay, individuals are usually dissatisfied if they feel that their treatment is inequitable.

Further, depending on expectations, more money does not necessarily lead to satisfaction. "For example, if one anticipates a 6 percent increase in salary but receives only a 2 percent increase, he may be pushed toward dissatisfaction even though he has received more pay" (Cohen 1974, p. 371).

The high cost of living in an area can also be a reason for dissatisfaction with one's salary (Morse 1953). For example, an assistant professor teaching and living in an area where the cost of living is high might be dissatisfied with a salary of $26,000 because the amount of pay is meager compared to the cost of living for the area. An assistant professor teaching and living in a small, rural community, however, might be satisfied with making $26,000 if the cost of living for that area is low.

Dissatisfaction with work also occurs when people believe they should receive more money for the type and amount of work accomplished (Morse 1953). For example, full-time professors in a college of medicine might believe they should receive more money than professors in a college of education because of the nature of their profession. Likewise, professors of medicine can perceive the demands for the preparation of their courses as being more exacting because of the life-and-death nature of their work.

Employees can be dissatisfied because their salary is low compared to similar jobs in the same organization (Morse 1953). A full professor of biology at a small college might receive a lower salary than a full professor of chemistry at the same institution, and the professor of biology can be dissatisfied for that reason. People can become dissatisfied when they believe they should receive more compensation because of their education, experience, and/or length of service (Morse 1953). For example, a professor in an English department with a Ph.D., 15 years of teaching experience, numerous publications, and 10 years of service might expect a higher salary than a professor who has an M.A. degree, 10 years of teaching experience, only a few publications, and five years of service.

Certainly, because salary can affect job satisfaction, the mechanism for determining compensation (for example, merit pay) will also affect a faculty member's job satisfaction. But merit pay by itself does not necessarily provide an incentive for productivity.

. . . because salary can affect job satisfaction, the mechanism for determining compensation . . . will also affect a faculty member's job satisfaction.

Merit systems assume that money is the "bottom line" of employee satisfaction—that more money will mean a more productive faculty. . . . Many underpaid yet hardworking faculty have shown that this is not necessarily true and that salary, while certainly a motivator, is only one such motivator (Fassiotto 1986, p. 15).

Because faculty salaries did not keep up with the Consumer Price Index from about 1970 to 1982, instead of merit, perhaps one should look at the demerits of the situation (Dennis 1982). Furthermore:

Many merit systems are based on the rather out-of-date management assumption that the employees are essentially lazy, that only a few are truly meritorious. It is quite possible and even probable that many faculty members do quite a bit more than the minimum . . . to make life at an institution better for all. . . . If a merit system is designed to affect the "negligent and unworthy," it ceases to be a merit system and becomes a system of punishment (Fassiotto 1986, pp. 14–15).

Thus, when the variable of merit pay is introduced, enhanced job satisfaction does not necessarily occur as expected.

Tenure

Another correlate of job satisfaction is tenure, which has been described as job security (Bowen and Schuster 1986; Saunders 1990).

A faculty member on tenure has a commitment from the employing institution, barring exceptional circumstances, that he may hold his position throughout his career until retirement. However, in practice, tenure is part of a wider contractual system that relates to academic freedom and to the participation of peers in personnel decisions involving faculty (Bowen and Schuster 1986, p. 235).

"Attainment of these status symbols [tenure and a faculty member's standing on the graduate faculty] would lead to higher levels of job satisfaction. Receiving these honors indicates that one has been successful in his work. There is also a certain amount of prestige associated with them" (Sprague 1974, p. 21). In reality, while tenure relates to both economic security and academic freedom, it is discussed here only from the perspective of job security. A study of nontenured faculty members at an urban, public university found that a positive relationship existed between job security and job satisfaction (Luu 1985). While job security is, in fact, a facet of job satisfaction:

*The resulting high correlation coefficient may also be attrib-
uted to the peculiar characteristics of the academy as an
enterprise, where tenure (job security) is both a low level
need—a necessary condition for job satisfaction—and a
self-actualization need—a sufficient condition for job satisfaction* (Luu 1985, pp. 58–59).

Many faculty members are tenured. In 1989–90, 63.5 percent
of all faculty were tenured, with 69.7 percent of the men
tenured and 48.5 percent of the women (U.S. Dept. of Education 1991) (see table 1).

TABLE 1

FULL-TIME INSTRUCTIONAL FACULTY WITH TENURE
(Institutions Reporting Tenure Status by Academic Rank during Academic Year 1989-90)

Academic Rank	Percent with Tenure
Professors	95.6
Associate professors	81.0
Assistant professors	19.7
Instructors	6.9
Lecturers	7.8

Source: U.S. Dept. of Education 1991, p. 229, table 223.

Tenured and nontenured faculty exhibited significant differences on three subscales of the Job Descriptive Index (JDI)
(Sprague 1974). Nontenured faculty members were significantly less satisfied than were tenured faculty on the subscales Work on the Present Job, Present Pay, and Coworkers.
"In every case the nontenured faculty had lower mean satisfaction scores than tenured faculty" (p. 87). Other studies
found similar results: "Teacher educators who are tenured
are more satisfied than nontenured teacher education faculty"
(Wolfson 1986, p. 86). Tenured faculty, in a study of faculty
in the General College at the University of Minnesota, were
relatively satisfied with security, reporting a higher mean score
than tenure-track and nontenured faculty on the security scale
of the Minnesota Satisfaction Questionnaire (MSQ) (Grahn
et al. 1981). A study of 426 teacher educators in 39 public and
25 private institutions found that the mean for work satisfac-

tion for tenured faculty was significantly higher than the mean for nontenured faculty (Nussel, Wiersma, and Rusche 1988). And a survey using the Minnesota Satisfaction Questionnaire short form found no statistically significant difference in the perceptions of full-time faculty members at selected southern institutions regarding job satisfaction and tenure status (Ibrahim 1985).[2]

Faculty Rank

Faculty rank is a variable of job satisfaction closely related to age (Sprague 1974). (See table 2 for the number of professors by gender and overall for certain ranks.) "Even though there is little in the higher education literature, professorial rank might be compared to differing organizational levels in other kinds of organizations" (Sprague 1974, p. 19). The higher one's level in an organization is, the greater his or her job satisfaction will be (Herzberg, Mausner, and Snyderman 1959), which is not surprising, given that "a number of other satisfaction-related job factors are implied by higher levels, such as responsibility, money, prestige, and more intrinsically rewarding work" (Harrison 1979, p. 20).

TABLE 2

**FULL-TIME INSTRUCTIONAL FACULTY IN
INSTITUTIONS OF HIGHER EDUCATION (Fall 1985)**

Academic Rank	Women	Men	Total
Professors	15,011	114,258	129,269
Associate professors	25,936	85,156	111,092
Assistant professors	39,845	71,463	111,308
Instructors	32,160	43,251	75,411
Lecturers	4,668	5,098	9,766
Other faculty	10,443	16,783	27,226
Total	128,063	336,009	464,072

Source: U.S. Dept. of Education 1991, p. 219, table 212.

---

2. While one survey of university faculty in the United States (Winkler 1982) found no difference in the level of job satisfaction for tenured university faculty and nontenured university faculty using the Job Descriptive Index (JDI) and the Minnesota Satisfaction Questionnaire (MSQ), the JDI was not validated for use of a total score and subscale scores should have been used rather than a total score for the analysis (P. Cain Smith 22 May 1989, personal communication).

In one study, full professors reported the highest level of job satisfaction and assistant professors the lowest (Winkler 1982). In another, "academic rank and satisfaction were related in that higher-ranked faculty expressed greater satisfaction" (Steen, Giunipero, and Newgren 1985, p. 351): The level of satisfaction by faculty rank on a scale of one to five was 3.83 for instructors, 3.89 for assistant professors, 4.08 for associate professors, and 4.36 for full professors.

A study of industrial arts/technology teacher educators found significant differences in mean scores for job satisfaction between full professors (43.60) and assistant professors (41.58) (Wolfson 1986). Interestingly, the instructors' mean score (41.85) was higher than both the mean scores for assistant (41.58) and associate (41.62) professors. Another researcher found that instructors reported the highest levels of satisfaction for authority, co-workers, creativity, recognition, responsibility, social status, supervision–human relations, and supervision–technical relations (Grahn et al. 1981). "It may be that because instructors are new on the job and fresh and enthusiastic, their levels of satisfaction are very high" (p. 15). A study of full-time faculty members in selected southern universities, however, found that faculty members did not differ significantly in their perceptions regarding job satisfaction when they were compared by rank (Ibrahim 1985).

Supervision
"Supervision and the general style of leadership throughout the organization are usually much more important in influencing results than such general factors as attitudes toward the company and interest in the job itself" (Likert 1961, p. 25). Furthermore, "the kind of supervision used in the organization [has] an effect upon employees' job satisfaction" (Harrison 1979, p. 11). In fact, studies have indicated that employees like supervisors who are considerate (Vroom 1964) (meaning "behavior indicative of friendship, mutual trust, respect, and warmth in the relationship between the leader and the members of his staff" [Halpin 1959, p. 4]) and "employee-centered" (Likert 1961).

Leaders who are described as employee-oriented [or employee-centered] stress the relationship aspects of their job. They feel that every employee is important and take interest in everyone, accepting their individuality and per-

sonal needs. Production orientation [the other concept identified] emphasizes production and the technical aspects of the job; employees are seen as tools to accomplish the goals of the organization (Hersey and Blanchard 1988, p. 92).

"Supervisors with the best records of performance focus their primary attention on the human aspects of their subordinates' problems and on endeavoring to build effective work groups with high performance goals" (Likert 1961, p. 7), making them "employee-centered" supervisors. The faculty of baccalaureate degree nursing programs, for example:

. . . Expressed increased job satisfaction when they perceived positive socioemotional relations among faculty (e.g., intimacy), a minimum of formal, nomothetic behavior on the part of the dean/chairperson (e.g., aloofness), and humane treatment of the faculty by the dean/chairperson (e.g., consideration) (Hickman 1986, p. 104).

Supervisors who have the most favorable and cooperative attitudes in their work groups are supportive, friendly, helpful, kind but firm, and nonthreatening, display a genuine interest in the well-being of subordinates and a willingness to treat people sensitively and considerately, and are confident in the integrity, ability, and motivations of subordinates rather than suspicious and distrustful (Likert 1961). Individuals "value managers who are considerate of them as individuals, who show respect for them, who are honest, communicative, and allow some participation in making decisions" (Locke, Fitzpatrick, and White 1983, p. 345). One study found that faculty members' length of time at an institution played a role in their satisfaction: Those "who had been at the university 16 years or over were the most satisfied with supervision. Those . . . who had been at the university eight to 15 years were the least satisfied with supervision" (Sprague 1974, pp. 78–79).

Interpersonal Relationships
While interaction with a superior is critical to job satisfaction, interpersonal relationships with co-workers (subordinates or peers) arising when people interact in the performance of their jobs or "within working hours and on the premises of work but independent of the activities of the job" like during a coffee break (Herzberg, Mausner, and Snyderman 1959,

p. 47) could also affect one's job satisfaction (Harrison 1979). "The employee will be satisfied with agents in the situation (supervisors, subordinates, co-workers, management) to the degree that they are seen as facilitating the attainment of his work goals and work rewards, and to the degree that these agents are perceived as having important values in common with him" (Locke 1976, p. 1342).

Working Conditions
Working conditions refer to the physical environment (including ventilation, lighting, tools, space, and other similar environmental characteristics), the facilities of the institution, and the amount of work (Herzberg 1966). "With respect to working conditions, employees want convenience in terms of location and hours, resources that help them do their work effectively, and physical safety" (Locke, Fitzpatrick, and White 1983, p. 345). Unquestionably, poor working conditions often lead to job dissatisfaction.

The availability of laboratory and computer equipment, libraries, and statistical consulting centers are necessary support items and services for faculty members who intend to conduct research. In one study, 25.6 percent of the faculty identified job conditions (including equipment, facilities, and teaching schedules) as one of the chief dissatisfactions of college teaching (Diener 1984). An earlier study of job satisfaction found that faculty members were satisfied with their working conditions, including the number of classes or groups for which they were responsible, the number of hours they worked each week, their work schedule compared to that of people with similar training in other professions, their office facilities or work area, the adequacy of the instructional equipment they used, the number of course preparations required, and their work schedule compared to that of their co-workers (Seegmiller 1977). Another study found that those with 11 or more years of service had higher mean scores on the working conditions scale of the MSQ than those with 10 or fewer years of service (Grahn et al. 1981).

Policies and Administration
In the consideration of job satisfaction, policies and administration are referred to as "dissatisfiers" (Herzberg 1972). Characteristics of overall company policy and administration fall into two categories.

*One involved the adequacy or inadequacy of company
organization and management. Thus, a situation can exist
in which a [person] has lines of communication crossing
in such a way that he does not really know for whom he
is working, in which he has inadequate authority for satisfactory completion of his task, or in which a company policy
is not carried out because of inadequate organization of
the work. The second kind of overall characteristic of the
company involved not inadequacy but the harmfulness or
the beneficial effects of the company's policies. [They] are
primarily personnel policies. When viewed negatively, these
policies are not described as ineffective, but rather as
"malevolent"* (Herzberg 1972, pp. 196–97).

Faculty want to participate in institutional decision making
and might leave an institution if such opportunities are
limited. Consequently, "it seems important that administrators
find ways to provide opportunities for faculty to influence
the policies of their institutions . . . " (Near and Sorcinelli
1986, p. 389).

Faculty are also conscious of the effectiveness of the individuals who lead the institution. In one study, 35 percent of
all professors cited "administration and administrators not
competent" as the reason for leaving their jobs (Brown 1967,
p. 162). A more recent study found that 29 percent of the faculty in Idaho's public two-year postsecondary vocational education institutions and 30 percent of the faculty in Idaho's
public four-year postsecondary vocational education institutions cited administration as a dissatisfier or identified it
as a factor contributing to their exceptionally bad feelings
about their job; administration was ranked number two in
both cases (Hilton 1985).

Person-Environment Fit

Organizations prefer to hire individuals who will best meet
the requirements of the job, can adapt to training and changes
in job demands, and will remain loyal and committed to the
organization; similarly, prospective employees seek out organizations where their particular abilities and skills closely
match what is required in the workplace. This relationship
or interaction between the organization and the employee
is commonly known as "person-environment fit," a theory
"proposed as a method for understanding the process of

adjustment between organizational members and their work environments" (Caplan 1987b, p. 249). The academic environment at colleges and universities must undoubtedly represent a good match between "the needs and abilities of the employee [faculty] and the corresponding resources of and demands from the work [collegiate] environment" (Caplan 1987a, p. 103).

Job characteristics represent one factor that could help determine the interaction and fit between the institution and the faculty member. "Job characteristics theory may be conceptualized as a model of person-environment fit [that] focuses on matching the characteristics of jobs to the abilities and needs of jobholders" (Kulik, Oldham, and Hackman 1987, p. 278).

> *Job characteristics theory posits that all three of the psychological states must be experienced by an individual if desirable outcomes are to emerge. First, the person must* experience the work as meaningful. *That is, the individual must feel that the work he or she does is generally worthwhile, valuable, or important by some system of values he or she accepts. Second, the individual must* experience personal responsibility *for work outcomes. The individual must feel personally accountable for the results of the work he or she does. Finally, the person must have* knowledge of the results of his or her work. *That is, the individual must know and understand, on a continuous basis, how effectively he or she is performing the job. If any one of these three states is not present, motivation and satisfaction will be attenuated* (Kulik, Oldham, and Hackman 1987, pp. 280–81).

The theory of person-environment fit helps explain the extent to which workers are successful in their particular environment, thus enhancing their overall job satisfaction. Colleges and universities that provide an environment conducive to the fulfilling of faculty members' psychological needs, allowing them to use their talents as they see fit and freeing them from contextual worries, are the institutions where faculty will be the most satisfied and the ones where they will want to continue working.

Collective Bargaining
"Collective bargaining arrangements in institutions of higher education have begun to replace the more traditional

employee-employer relationship" (Hill 1982, p. 165). Collective bargaining is now the mechanism for reaching agreement on policies regarding curriculum, grades, admissions, course scheduling, standards for matriculation, teaching methods, faculty hiring, tenure, sabbatical leaves, and decisions about promotion on many campuses (Douglas 1991, p. ix).

A study of the relationship between faculty job satisfaction and collective bargaining found that faculty in unionized institutions were significantly more satisfied with the economic, administrative, associational, and convenience dimensions of job satisfaction than those in nonunion institutions but that the two faculty groups were no different with regard to the teaching and recognition-support dimensions of their jobs (Hill 1982). "Collective bargaining does affect the level of job satisfaction of college faculty in a positive fashion, but the effects vary depending on the specific dimension of job satisfaction being considered" (p. 176). The results cannot be generalized to institutions of higher education throughout the United States, however, because the study was based on a sample of 20 Pennsylvania institutions, the unionized faculty involved in the study were drawn exclusively from four-year state colleges, and the conclusions were based on responses from only 45.5 percent (1,089 faculty members) of the individuals surveyed.

To determine whether collective bargaining impinges substantively on the job satisfaction of faculty in higher education, future research will have to address the situation in different types of institutions, in different parts of the country, and in colleges with various forms of collective bargaining arrangements. Certainly different conditions and situations may well affect the climate of job satisfaction among faculty (Hill 1982, p. 178).

A study of instructors, assistant professors, associate professors, and professors at the University of Oregon found that "those respondents who indicated they were dissatisfied with various conditions of their employment were significantly more inclined to indicate support for bargaining than were the respondents who were satisfied" (Feuille and Blandin 1974, p. 687). Faculty who expressed dissatisfaction with their current salary; their current fringe benefits; the representation of faculty interests in the campus administration, the state board of higher education, and the state legislature; and the existing personnel decision-making system "were significantly more likely to express a preference for the establishment of a faculty collective bargaining system than were those respondents who were satisfied with these same conditions" (p. 687).

A survey of faculty members and librarians at New York University found similar results (Bornheimer 1985). That study focused on the degree of satisfaction with six conditions—academic freedom, conditions of employment, educational policy, faculty personnel policy, financial benefits, and participation in governance—and on the respondents' support for unionization.

> *The higher the degree of satisfaction with conditions, the greater the probability that the faculty member voted for the No Representative position; the less satisfaction, the greater the chance that the faculty member voted for a change in existing conditions by supporting the . . . [NYU Federation of United Professionals]* (Bornheimer 1985, p. 296).

Although mediation is common in higher education (Birnbaum 1984), little has been written about its effectiveness. Nevertheless, one can assume that:

> *Even if the negotiation process [were] successfully concluded, the antagonisms, extreme positions, harsh rhetoric, and secretiveness of the table might affect other institutional relationships and programs. In the extreme, of course, adversarial bargaining could lead to threats, job actions, strikes, or other actions that might disrupt the learning process, lead to schisms among various campus groups, and create an environment of distrust, alienation, and decreased educational effectiveness* (Birnbaum 1984, p. 720).

Summary
Major factors in the workplace for faculty members in higher education include salary, tenure, rank, supervision, interpersonal relationships, working conditions, policies and administration, person-environment fit, and collective bargaining. Not surprisingly, salary appears to be one of the greatest sour-

ces of dissatisfaction with one's job (Edmundson 1969; Ladd 1979; Winkler 1982), but tenure and rank are important to faculty as well. A positive relationship exists between job security (tenure) and job satisfaction (Luu 1985), and higher-level faculty typically are more satisfied.

Individuals want to be supervised by respectful, considerate, employee-centered, honest, and fair men and women who are able to communicate effectively and are willing to involve employees in making decisions that affect their work and lives (Locke, Fitzpatrick, and White 1983, p. 345). But while the interaction with superiors is critical to one's satisfaction, relationships with subordinates or peers also affect it (Harrison 1979).

One important source of dissatisfaction for faculty members is their working conditions, including equipment, facilities, and teaching schedules (Diener 1984). Faculty could decide to leave higher education altogether as a result of poor working conditions, a problem that will likely be exacerbated in the future as fewer resources are available to support faculty and as money for equipment and renovation is frozen. In addition, some faculty view administration and certain administrators as less than highly competent, leading to feelings of dissatisfaction with the job in general. And collective bargaining agreements can affect a faculty member's job satisfaction in two ways: the working conditions stipulated in the agreement and the relationships that develop between faculty and administration during negotiations.

The importance of the person-environment fit cannot be overemphasized. The faculty member's needs, skills, and goals must "fit" the institution's expectations, resources, and policy directives. Thus, colleges and universities must be sure that expectations and rewards—and sanctions—are clearly delineated for faculty before they are hired so that a good "match" will result, increasing the likelihood of their retention and success as a faculty member.

Dissatisfaction with any of these factors can cause a faculty member to leave his or her job or discourage others from going into the field. Leaders of higher education institutions must take steps to enhance these conditions for faculty as a way of maintaining a quality, diverse faculty in the future.

WOMEN FACULTY

Women have played an important role in higher education faculty since at least the Civil War (Bowen and Schuster 1986) (even though men have always dominated the field of higher education), accounting for "about one-fourth of the full-time instructional staff in institutions of higher education" (Fuchs and Lovano-Kerr 1981, p. 4). Job satisfaction among women college professors, however, has been almost totally ignored by researchers (Hill 1984b), and it clearly deserves more attention (Hill 1983).

The appointment of women to faculty and administrative positions in significant numbers would go far toward establishing an environment conducive to women's success in a variety of arenas (Graham 1971). "The most important single observation about women in the academic world[, however,] is that their numbers decrease dramatically as the importance of the post increases" (Graham 1973, p. 163). Today, women typically represent a small percentage of the faculty cohort, hold the lower professorial ranks, work in part-time rather than full-time positions, represent disciplines typically considered reserved for females, work in less prestigious institutions, and are not tenured.

While some discrepancies exist in the numbers and corresponding percentages reported by various researchers, it is painfully clear that the representation of women on college and university faculties is, and always has been, relatively small. Women filled approximately 26 percent of all faculty positions in higher education in 1920. By the beginning of the 1930s, women represented 27 percent of the faculty, but the percentage declined to 22 percent in the 1960s (Cox 1982; Dean 1986; Halcomb 1979; Reskin and Phipps 1988), although it grew to 28 percent by 1970, 34 percent by 1980, and 35 percent by the mid-1980s (Reskin and Phipps 1988). "The picture is even bleaker for minority women, who represented 3 percent of all full-time faculty in 1976, with [African-American] women accounting for 2 percent, Asian women 0.4 percent, Hispanic women 0.4 percent, and Native American women less than 0.1 percent" (Simeone 1987, p. 29). Not surprisingly, women faculty members are clustered in traditionally "feminine" disciplines, such as English, education, foreign language, nursing, home economics, fine arts, social work, and library or archival sciences (Carnegie Commission 1973; Etaugh 1984; B. Freeman 1977; Gappa and Uehling 1979; Graham 1971; Reskin and Phipps 1988). Between 1974 and 1982,

... it is painfully clear that the representation of women on college and university faculties is, and always has been, relatively small.

the greatest percentage increase for the disciplines in which women were employed occurred in the field of psychology (5.2 percent), the smallest in engineering (1.7 percent) (Etaugh 1984).

The number of women who earn Ph.D.s in the physical sciences continues to be low, even though significant gains have been made recently. A disquieting statistic for higher education is that the number of doctorates earned by African-American women faculty between 1978 and 1988 increased by only 14 percent, whereas "the number of American Indian, Asian, and Hispanic women receiving doctorates increased by at least 70 percent . . . " ("Ph.D.s for Women" 1990, p. 4).

In addition, as the prestige of an institution increases, the number of women faculty members declines. Relatively few women faculty members work at highly selective research universities (Carnegie Commission 1973; Farley 1982; Hill 1984b) or doctoral-degree-granting institutions with a strong research orientation or with scientific and technical curricula. In fact, women faculty are "located disproportionately in two-year and four-year state colleges—where teaching loads are heavy and administrative demands are high . . . rather than in major universities with the research resources and opportunities that support publication upon which academic eminence and recognition are based" (Fox 1984, p. 247).

Job Satisfaction, Women, and the Workplace

Interestingly, and perhaps stereotypically, "the generally accepted proposition involving job satisfaction of women is that they are significantly less satisfied than men" (Ivancevich and Donnelly 1968, p. 174). Among young workers from 21 to 29 years of age, "in general, women workers are significantly more likely to report dissatisfaction than are male workers. This was true among all age groups, but the gap between men and women was least among younger workers" (Sheppard and Herrick 1972, p. 117). A study of male and female plant workers found that female workers tended to be somewhat less satisfied with their jobs than their male counterparts (Hulin and Smith 1964).

Even in academia, a study of community college faculty members found that female teaching professionals reported less overall job satisfaction, specifically, significantly "less liking of their current job situations and less opportunity to do what they are best at than their male counterparts" (Hollon and Gemmill 1976, p. 89). Another study of college faculty concluded that "using either . . . [the Job Descriptive Index or the Minnesota Satisfaction Questionnaire], the female respondents indicated less job satisfaction than the male respondents" (Winkler 1982, p. 99). Others, however, found no significant differences in the level of job satisfaction between male and female educators (Wolfson 1986).

Nearly one-third of the female professors in one study believed that they had been the victims of discrimination in salary and one-fourth that they had been discriminated against in terms of "the status accorded to them" (Mayfield and Nash 1976, p. 633). Additionally, 25 percent indicated that performance standards were higher for them than for their male counterparts. In the same study, "the area of difficulty most frequently encountered by women (40 percent responded to this alternative) was with regard to the need to prove their capabilities before being accepted by male colleagues" (p. 633). Surprisingly, despite the discrimination and the higher standards against which they are judged, 92 percent of the 40 respondents said they would still choose the same job.

In an early study that focused on gender and ethnicity, the "well-documented tendency of [African-American] males to report lower job satisfaction apparently extends to [African-American] female employees" (Weaver 1974, p. 49). Unfortunately, it appears that when gender and ethnicity are combined, African-American women appear to be less satisfied than both their white female counterparts and their African-American male colleagues.

The impact of gender on overall job satisfaction and productivity is difficult to determine because conflicting results have emerged from the few research studies conducted. Perhaps more can be learned about the effect of gender on job satisfaction by looking at specific internal stressors, factors in the workplace, and life-style stressors that come into play when women work outside the home.

Internal Stressors
Internal stressors are the subjective, internally motivating aspects of life that add to or detract from job satisfaction. While it has been suggested that "in general, intrinsic [internal] aspects of the job appear to be more important to men than to women" (Herzberg et al. 1957, p. 72), both women

and men value internal factors over ones in the workplace (Saleb and Lalljee 1969). Again, no conclusive evidence suggests that gender affects the way internal factors are valued; therefore, it is important to look at various rewards and the role that gender plays in job satisfaction or dissatisfaction. For purposes of this discussion, the following internal stressors are explored: teaching, research, achievement, and recognition for achievement.

Teaching and research

Women typically teach more hours than men (Austin and Gamson 1983), and women faculty "bear a disproportionate share of undergraduate instruction, have less contact with graduate students, and are less likely to be given teaching assistants" than their male colleagues (B. Freeman 1977, p. 177). In fact, "women . . . are in many cases little more than faculty teaching assistants. They tend to do the hard, boring work of handling large introductory courses, while their better-paid, higher-ranked male colleagues teach the more exciting and professionally rewarding, upper-level undergraduate and graduate courses" (p. 178). They also usually have more students to advise, thus further diminishing the time available for scholarship. Further:

> Because of their small numbers, Hispanic women faculty members are even more overburdened than white faculty women—especially with advising Hispanic and other minority students and numerous committee assignments—thus limiting their time for research and publishing (Nieves-Squires 1991, p. 5).

Women are not as involved in publishing as their male colleagues, perhaps because they are clustered in disciplines that are more likely to be oriented toward practice, with rewards that are not associated with research and scholarship. And unfortunately, "if academic women are less involved and less productive in research, in the area in which they focus the lion's share of their effort—teaching—they appear to be no more effective overall than their male colleagues" (Finkelstein 1987, p. 84).

"Faculty members often receive mixed signals about how to allocate their energies among research, teaching, and service to achieve tenure . . . [, and] the strain is greatest when research-oriented faculty are pushed to teach and teaching-oriented faculty are pressured to do more research" (Austin and Gamson 1983, p. 17). Faculty who have heavier teaching loads experience more pressure in terms of meeting their job demands (Schultz and Chung 1988). Interestingly, "natural scientists had the lowest teaching loads and the least role conflict; humanities and social science faculty carried heavier teaching loads and experienced greater role strain" (Austin and Gamson 1983, p. 18). Clearly, women are more heavily represented in the humanities and social sciences—little wonder that the teaching role is a burden for women faculty.

Achievement and recognition for achievement
"The area of difficulty most frequently encountered by women [in one study] was with regard to the need to prove their capabilities before being accepted by male colleagues" (Mayfield and Nash 1976, p. 633).

> Women professionals in comparison to their male counterparts are significantly more frequently bothered by the feeling that: (1) they are not fully qualified to handle their jobs; (2) they have too heavy a workload; (3) the amount of work they have to do interferes with how well it gets done; and (4) they cannot get information needed to carry out their jobs (Hollon and Gemmill 1976, p. 86).

In addition, women faculty are less satisfied with their positions and experience more job-related tension than male faculty.

"The bulk of research indicates that women are likely to be evaluated more harshly than men, particularly in traditionally male areas. They are seen as having less authority, and their opinions are accepted less readily" (Simeone 1987, p. 74). And, not surprisingly, "women in male sex-typed units of business and law express less satisfaction with their work on the present job" (Wissman 1988, p. 41). In effect, women are caught in a double bind when it comes to the approach they take to their work.

> Caught between two sets of rules, women cannot avoid running afoul of one of them. If they seek to practice a profession by following the rules and habits long established by its male practitioner—competition, aggression—they

offend the old conventions defining womanly virtue. But if women behave in a professional milieu according to the old female norms, if they are patient, deferential, accommodating, smiling, soft-spoken, they appear weak (Aisenberg and Harrington 1988, p. 18).

Factors in the Workplace

"On all measures of formal status [factors in the workplace,] women lag behind men" (Simeone 1987, p. 34); however, it is important to explore specific variables affecting women faculty to determine whether this statement still holds true in the 1990s. This subsection explores those incentives or disincentives external to faculty members—salary, tenure, academic rank, interpersonal relationships, working conditions—and their relationship to the gender of the instructor and job satisfaction.

Salary

Even though the gap is narrowing, when it comes to compensation, "women are paid less than men, even after controlling for rank, institutional type, and discipline" (Finkelstein 1987, p. 69). When men's and women's salaries were compared by category, affiliation, and rank for the 1991–92 academic year, in all cases, the average salaries for women were lower than the average salaries for men. When the categories and affiliations were combined, the average salary at the professorial level for men was $59,180, whereas it was $52,380 for women; at the associate professor level, men earned $44,130 and women made $41,040; at the assistant professor level, men were paid $37,240 and women received $34,380; at the instructor level, the average salary for men was $28,220 and $26,390 for women; at the lecturer level, men made $32,800, while women earned $28,530 (American Association of University 1992).

While job satisfaction of women faculty and salary levels have not been the subject of much scrutiny, research data about female university administrators could shed some light on the subject. "Salary was found to have a significantly negative relationship when compared to role conflict, internal self-esteem, and external self-esteem" of females who served as administrators in a university setting (Anderson 1984, p. 95). Consequently, female university administrators who receive "low salaries" might be less satisfied with their administrative work than those who receive "high salaries." Perhaps, then, women faculty who are paid less than their male counterparts might also feel less satisfied with their work in academia because the rewards do not reflect the perceived level or intensity of their contributions. But:

Among men and women in the same income ranges, differences in work dissatisfaction tended to disappear. So much for the job dissatisfaction problem among women! The theoretical solution is simple: equal employment opportunity! (Sheppard and Herrick 1972, p. 8).

Tenure

Because women are typically clustered in the lower academic ranks, they are also less likely to have been granted tenure; subsequently, "they are likely to experience much more sharply than males a sense of job insecurity" (B. Freeman 1977, p. 177). Today, in effect, a smaller percentage of women are tenured compared to a decade ago. Specifically, in 1980–81, 49.7 percent of the full-time women faculty were tenured, compared to 70 percent of the men faculty members. Today, while the percentage of male faculty members is the same, the percentage for women has dropped to 45.9 percent (American Association of University 1992). Further, women are tenured at a slower rate than their male counterparts (Astin and Snyder 1982). For instance, from 1972 to 1982, the proportion of tenured men increased by 17.7 percent, while the proportion of tenured women increased by only 13.4 percent.

Tenure status is also affected by the type of institution where a woman is employed, with discrepancies in tenure status of men and women greater at public institutions and universities than at two-year colleges and private institutions (Etaugh 1984).

Academic rank

As the academic rank increases from instructor to full professor, the percentage of women holding a particular rank steadily declines. For example, in the early 1970s only 9 percent of all full professors were women (Carnegie Commission 1973), and that percentage had increased only slightly, to 10 percent, by the mid-1980s (Fox and Hesse-Biber 1984; Fulton 1986). "In 1980–81, 70.7 percent of all women faculty were at or below the assistant professor rank or were unranked" (Finkelstein 1987, p. 69).

In the mid-1980s, 30 percent of all assistant professors and 50 percent of instructors were women, a situation providing some hope that, with promotions, women will soon hold academic rank equivalent with men. But "women are promoted at a slower rate than their male colleagues" (Finkelstein 1987, p. 69). Thus, it is understandable that a recent study found men faculty more satisfied with opportunities for promotion than women faculty (Logan 1990). Today, except for the levels of instructor and lecturer, women remain underrepresented in the academic ranks: Only 5.1 percent of women are full professors, compared to 31 percent of men, 7.7 percent of women are associate professors (19.9 percent of men), and 11.1 percent of women are assistant professors (15.8 percent of men) (American Association of University 1992).

A study of female faculty in traditional and nontraditional disciplines in the late 1980s found that, regardless of discipline, female full professors felt the most satisfied with work, followed by associate professors, assistant professors, and instructors (Crawford 1987). Furthermore, female full professors in the same study said they felt the most secure in their positions, again followed by associate professors, assistant professors, and instructors. Female full professors identified more strongly with their institutions and would not leave them as readily as would associate and assistant professors (Crawford 1987).

Interpersonal relationships

Interpersonal relationships are important factors in establishing an appropriate working environment and in motivating people to do a good job. While women are typically considered to be exceptionally good communicators, women faculty working in community colleges reported greater difficulty in communicating their ideas to superiors, felt that they were less influential in terms of the ultimate outcome of the superiors' decision, and said they were consulted less frequently than men faculty with whom they worked (Hollon and Gemmill 1976). Moreover, women typically are not permitted access to male networks that "effectively exclude women from meaningful participation in the affairs of their institutions and rob them of a sense of belonging" (Hill 1984b, p. 180). Unfortunately, "minority women are more likely than other women to be excluded from informal and social activities within their departments and institutions—sometimes by white women as well as by white and minority men" (Nieves-Squires 1991, p. 5).

Working conditions

Female instructors at community colleges in one study reported that they had less influence over their working conditions than their male colleagues (Hollon and Gemmill 1976). Interestingly, these same women faculty were less likely to "marry their jobs" or view their professions as the source of major satisfaction in their lives. Another study of women faculty found that females representing traditional and nontraditional fields in 12 of Ohio's state-assisted institutions generally perceived their working environments as satisfactory (Crawford 1987).

In terms of institutional setting, "women are generally more satisfied in institutions where the sexual composition reflects a 'less highly' male-dominated milieu" (Hill 1984b, p. 179). (This increased satisfaction, however, related only to the factors associated with the job setting.) An analysis of responses from 1,256 men and women faculty who had completed their highest degrees within the previous 10 years concluded that "women in applied fields were likely to be slightly more satisfied with their departments (1.06) and institutions (1.09) and women in pure fields slightly less satisfied with their departments (-1.61)" (Ethington, Smart, and Zeltmann 1989, p. 266). In selective liberal arts colleges, however, women in " 'pure' disciplines have atypically high departmental satisfaction (7.83), while women in 'applied' disciplines report uncommonly low levels of institutional satisfaction (-10.08)" (p. 268). The lower level of satisfaction with the institution might be the result of the inconsistency created between the applied nature of the discipline and the general focus of the institution.

When the job satisfaction of African-American women with their working conditions is considered, the situation is not very positive.

> *Black women, who have gained access to higher education and higher-paying positions, often find themselves in less than optimal work environments. The racist and sexist attitudes of colleagues can often result in less than satisfactory work conditions and increased stress in the life of the black female professional . . .* (Steward 1987, p. 3).

The fact that women from ethnic minority groups tend to experience even more difficulty operating in higher education than their white female counterparts could account for their inadequate representation among the faculty.

> *Discrimination against female professionals occurs when females of equivalent qualifications, experience, and performance as males do not share equally in the decision-making process [or] receive equal rewards[, such as] money, promotions, prestige, professional recognition, and honors* (Theodore 1971, p. 27).

Thus, women who are located in jobs at the lower echelons of the organizational hierarchy and make less money than their male colleagues could be dissatisfied. And "when there are but a few women on a faculty, excessive demands are made upon them; not only must each fulfill the usual academic requirements but she must serve as the token woman on all kinds of committees" (Graham 1971, p. 733). Certainly, this fact alone creates overload and job-related distress.

Selected groups of women faculty employed at research and doctoral-degree-granting institutions have "unusually low levels of institutional and departmental dissatisfaction" (Ethington, Smart, and Zeltmann 1989, p. 267). Consequently, on the one hand, institutional officials at research and doctoral-degree-granting institutions need to pay attention to the factors that contribute to or detract from the job satisfaction of the few women faculty they now employ if they wish to retain them. On the other hand, leaders at other types of institutions need to continue to monitor the job satisfaction of the women faculty at their institutions to ensure that rewards are readily available.

Life-style Stressors
To the uninformed, the illusion persists that faculty members in colleges and universities are engaged in one of the least stressful occupations around; faculty have flexible working hours, leave home at odd times during the day, appear at their children's school functions during "normal" working hours, and are on campus for seemingly only a few hours. Not necessarily: "Academics have more flexible work schedules but are less able to leave their work at the office" (Biernat and Wortman 1991, p. 846). Moreover, one of the greatest chal-

lenges faculty face is the balancing of endless academic responsibilities with their personal lives (Austin and Pilat 1990). The relationship between job and home could be a condition of "seamlessness" that could "allow the job to become obtrusive and all-consuming" (Sorcinelli and Near 1989, p. 59). In effect:

Faculty members are likely to spend large amounts of time working at home. They tie vacations to their work by scheduling them to coincide with leaves or conferences, voraciously read within and outside their discipline, and tend to socialize with other academics (Sorcinelli and Near 1989, p. 59).

In reality, most faculty work quite hard, an average of at least 50 hours each week (Clark, Corcoran, and Lewis 1986); however, "women faculty are likely to work 80 or more hours per week" (Hensel 1991, p. 49). Thirty-five of these hours are focused on housework and children; compared to men, who average seven hours per week in the home, women are clearly at a disadvantage (Hensel 1990). When the family includes small children, the woman's work week is astronomical. Women in working couples without children or whose children have left the nest spend five to nine hours more per week on housework than their husbands, but when infants and preschoolers enter the picture, women work 16 to 24 hours more per week than men. Women who have children under the age of three work an average of 90 hours per week (Scarr, Phillips, and McCartney 1989).

Women who have children under the age of three work an average of 90 hours per week.

While all faculty members in higher education have to balance their personal and professional lives, women faculty usually have primary responsibility for multiple "jobs" (spouse, parent, teacher, researcher, committee member, mentor, adviser, housekeeper, cook, and chauffeur, to name a few) and often have to give up leisure time and sleep (Hensel 1991; Sorcinelli and Near 1989) to meet the needs of others.

Women do not have a wife at home who will handle housekeeping and child care responsibilities. Nor do they have a wife who devotes a significant portion of her time to her mate's career. If a woman is married, it is likely that her husband has a career of his own and has little time to support his wife's career. . . . It is said that a professorship is a two-person career. When a woman is in the position, it is a one-person career and the one person may be psychologically divided between home and career (Hensel 1991, p. 9).

Although "stress can be the spice of life, if we handle it right" (Gmelch 1988, p. 139), life-style stressors, when left unchecked, often lead to burnout, overload, imbalance, ulcers, and heart disease. Many researchers "equate burnout with stress, connect burnout with an endless list of adverse health and well-being variables, and suggest it is caused by the relentless pursuit of success" (Burke 1987, p. 252). Frequently, "emotional exhaustion" is the primary cause of burnout (Burke 1987).

Unfortunately, women faculty can rarely expect consolation and/or assistance from their colleagues or their institutions, because the majority of higher education's leaders (typically white, married males) have never had to deal with such overwhelmingly complex life-styles. Thus, it is important to identify the primary life-style stressors that add complications to the lives of women faculty. Unfortunately, little information exists when it comes to the stressors women faculty in higher education experience (Gmelch, Lovrich, and Wilke 1984; Gmelch, Wilke, and Lovrich 1986), and more research in this area is definitely needed. "This panel of variables [extraorganizational ones, including the interaction of family, life, and organizational stress] is almost never examined. Instead each life domain is treated as a closed system and the interaction of work and family has been largely ignored" (Burke 1987, p. 258). It is hoped that, when armed with empirical evidence from future research studies, institutional officials will begin working to identify ways of providing services and support so more women will choose teaching as a career.

Family demands
The relationship between work and family can be described in three different ways (Glowinkowski and Cooper 1987). First, *spillover* occurs when events at work affect the family and vice versa; in most instances, spillover into family matters occurs when the environment at work is negative. In effect, "when work was important to an individual, conflict between the two environments was more likely than when work was less important. . . . When work is not important, there will

be less spillover of negative work outcomes" (p. 190). Second, *compensation* could occur when the individual attempts to make up for deficits in one area by maximizing the other. Third, some people manage to keep work and family relationships *independent* (or segmented [Sorcinelli and Near 1989]). Given the desire of women faculty to succeed in their chosen profession, it is easy to see why family and work issues tend to overlap.

Clearly, having a spouse and one child, or several children, creates demands on men and women faculty alike, but the pressures that women face are decidedly greater (Glowinkowski and Cooper 1987), because society still considers them primarily responsible for the family. If it were easy to balance the competing demands of work and family, more women with families would have been promoted to full professor and to executive-level positions in higher education, but very few successful women (but most successful men) are married with children (Hensel 1991). When women challenge tradition and try to combine work and family, depression often results, because "employed mothers feel a more intense sense of responsibility or guilt with respect to their children's problems" (Baruch, Biener, and Barnett 1987, p. 133).

Unfortunately, "equal status outside the home seems not to translate into equal sharing of responsibilities within the home and . . . women, more than men, are critical of their performances as spouses and parents" (Biernat and Wortman 1991, p. 858). Ironically, men often feel more positive about their wives' parenting and abilities as spouses than women, and men are more often positive about their wives' ability to balance their multiple roles than women.

Marriage and family are easier for men to handle.

If women bear primary responsibility for the family, that responsibility is reduced for men, leaving their side of the personal/professional equation relatively manipulable. Men, even if married and with children, can increase or decrease their civic responsibilities, cultural pursuits, even engagement in family affairs to adjust to demands of "the work."
. . . Thus, what is for men a matter of tension between two realms, a conflict requiring shifting emphases and continuing compromise, becomes for women more nearly a choice

—either "the life" or "the work" (Aisenberg and Harrington 1988, p. 108).

Marriage and children. Clearly, marriage and children add numerous dilemmas to the professional equation for women faculty. "Marriage is bad for women's careers" (Crawford 1982, p. 90) and a point of contention that creates inner struggles and conflicts for women professionals (Amatea and Cross 1981; Benton 1986; Crawford 1982; Villadsen and Tack 1981). Not only do women have to be concerned about their responsibilities for domestic chores and society's stereotypical views of a "woman's place," but they also must perform expertly in all dimensions of the faculty position. Moreover, "the monetary success of a professionally employed wife thus seems to carry a price: the loss of perceived competence as a spouse in both partners" (Biernat and Wortman 1991, p. 854).

Competing claims of the personal and the professional realms loom in prospect for the young woman, take a bewildering variety of shapes while a career is in progress, and finally form a pattern that prods the older woman to ask whether she had made the right choices (Aisenberg and Harrington 1988, p. 107).

Professional women have experimented with a variety of strategies for handling "the life and the work," for example, marrying early or marrying late after establishing themselves in "the work." Some women choose simply to deal with "the work" by forfeiting marriage and children entirely (Aisenberg and Harrington 1988; Marshall and Jones 1990). Women who choose to marry and have children are often "forced to lead two separate entire lives simultaneously. . . . They end up squeezing two lives into one through superhuman effort" (Aisenberg and Harrington 1988, p. 117). These women simply have to hope that personal or family illness or financial problems do not surface because they have no margin of error.

Dual-career families. Typically, "the family follows the man because traditional mores dictate that he is the principal wage earner" (Aisenberg and Harrington 1988, p. 124). Women, on the other hand, are often unable to capitalize on opportunities to advance their careers because of geographic immobility created by the priority placed on their husbands' careers (Marwell, Rosenfeld, and Spelerman 1979; Sagaria 1988), and changes in position "are the principal mechanism for increasing earnings, status, and authority" (Sagaria 1988, p. 305). If women are unable to relocate, their chances of increased job satisfaction and career advancement diminish substantially. Although in some nontraditional marriages the husband follows the wife's career, he often loses prestige and opportunities for advancement because of his willingness to support his wife's ambitions. Sadly, some suggest that couples are happiest when the man's career takes precedence (Biernat and Wortman 1991).

Another stressor on a dual-career marriage is the competitive spirit that often exists between the partners. Frequently, if the woman is more successful than her husband, tension erupts, fed by societal norms that do not give women the right to "trample on the image of the subordinate wife by forging ahead of the husband" (Sekaran 1986, p. 30). In probably more instances than have been documented, women compromise advancement in their careers to eliminate risks to their marriages and families. While healthy competition can be energizing and increase productivity, left unchecked, competition can be a major problem for dual-career couples.

Men and women faculty in dual-career marriages in one study turned to relatives, typically their own spouses, for support (Lloyd et al. 1982). Not surprisingly, other dual-career couples tended to be involved in their own networks but also relied on single people, couples where only one spouse worked, and dual-career couples. Interestingly, husbands' satisfaction with the marriage was linked to the supportiveness of the network, whereas for wives it was related to closeness and satisfaction with the network. "Perhaps the presence of network support helps to 'make up' for this decreased spousal support for the husband and thus helps to enhance his feelings of satisfaction" (Lloyd et al. 1982, p. 11).

The commuting marriage. The dual-career marriage frequently transforms itself into a commuting marriage so both spouses can enjoy the benefits of a successful professional career. In 1982, an estimated 700,000 couples were involved in commuting arrangements, with more than half of them involving academics, and "the percentage is probably continuing to grow" (Hileman 1990, p. 119). The widespread inci-

dence of commuting relationships in academia is predictable, given flexible scheduling that affords summer and intermittent vacations so couples can spend some sustained time together.

Because some institutions of higher education have rules concerning nepotism that prevent husbands and wives from being employed at the same college or university, commuting marriages are often the only vehicle available for both spouses to find fulfilling jobs in their areas of specialization (Hileman 1990). Typically, the woman benefits the most from the commuting life-style—and it is she who bears the brunt of the social stigma for not being a "traditional" wife.

In addition to representing a "socially deviant" life-style, a commuting marriage creates enormous emotional and financial costs too high for most married couples to manage. The emotional costs are frequently associated with the feelings of loneliness and anxiety created by lengthy periods of physical separation, problems associated with their reacquaintance as a married couple, particularly for women, and the absence of a support structure of friends and family because the couple wants to spend available time together rather than surrounded by others (Hileman 1990). In effect, most commuting couples compartmentalize their lives by focusing solely on work when they are apart and exclusively on each other when they are together. Finances are frequently a major issue, for the couple maintains two separate residences, spends thousands of dollars on travel, and pays extraordinarily high telephone bills to keep up with each other.

While the divorce rate for commuting couples is no higher than for couples who live together, men are typically more dissatisfied with the commuting life-style than are women (Hileman 1990). Perhaps this phenomenon can be explained by the facts that men in commuting relationships have to handle more domestic tasks (which they frequently dislike) and that they are not as likely as women to establish new friendships when they live alone.

Household responsibilities
When asked who took care of the household and who did the outdoor maintenance, "an encouraging one-quarter of men [recorded] themselves as contributing equally, [but] three-quarters of all women [had] to add major domestic responsibility to their other work, thus reducing the hours available for reading, writing, research, or professional updat-

ing" (Wilson and Byrne 1987, p. 137)—certainly important activities in the academic environment.

How do faculty in a dual-career marriage handle household chores? Women usually spend more time on such tasks:

Tasks are divided along traditional lines in these couples: Wives spend significantly more time than husbands . . . on child care, laundry, meal preparation, housekeeping, and food shopping; husbands spend significantly more time with lawn care (Seeborg 1990, p. 78).

Regardless, husbands are more likely to spend time on household tasks than they are on child care (Biernat and Wortman 1991). As the woman's educational level and income increase, the difference in time spent on household chores by both husband and wife decreases (Seeborg 1990). This change in responsibilities could occur because women have more "power" in the family by virtue of their increased educational and financial status or because they married nontraditional husbands (Sekaran 1986).

Child care
Women cannot resolve the conflict between home and career without a supportive husband and a fulfilling job; interestingly, male professors more frequently "engage in mutually supportive behaviors" than males in other professions (Sekaran 1986, p. 37). Nevertheless, "a husband's time at work is the strongest and most consistent associate of child-care involvement of both spouses and of the wife's relative to her husband's" (Biernat and Wortman 1991, p. 856). When fathers are involved in child care, they are usually "babysitting" (a term mothers rarely use when describing their involvement with their children) or most likely involved in "interactive play" with them (Biernat and Wortman 1991). Moreover, when children are part of the equation, husbands seem more willing to help around the house:

Children may be the main hindrance to a faculty member's research productivity[, for] children's needs cannot be postponed in favor of deadlines, as is the case with housekeeping or laundry. Thus, a supportive spouse is especially important for a faculty member with children (Seeborg 1990, p. 82).

As the earnings of the woman faculty member increase, a subsequent decrease occurs in the man's involvement in child care, perhaps as a result of the woman's guilt and her resulting desire to make up for this disparity in income. While modern fathers appear to be more involved and responsible for the care of their children than in the past, they are still involved primarily on the periphery (Biernat and Wortman 1991; Sekaran 1986).

Elder care

"In addition to career responsibilities, elder care is being added to the woman's traditional role of wife, mother, and homemaker" (Anglis 1990, p. 59). Middle-aged daughters are assuming the responsibility of caring for elderly parents, a situation that has added significant commitments of time to their already busy schedules (Archbold 1983; Brody et al. 1987; Naisbitt and Aburdene 1990; Sherman, Ward, and LaGory 1988; Winfield 1987). Women in their mid-40s to mid-50s are referred to as the "sandwich generation," frequently having to care for both young children at home and elderly parents in distant cities who need time and attention—a situation that adds conflicting demands on an already overcrowded life-style.

Physical and mental health

"Accumulating roles [seems] to have health benefits, up to some point. Women with few roles or with numerous ones [tend] to have poorer health than women with 'several'" (Verbrugge 1983, p. 17). Multiple roles do not automatically mean role conflict (Thoits 1983); in fact, "the lowest levels [of stress] are found among women who have the most complex role configuration, i.e., those who are simultaneously married, employed, and parents" (Kandel, Davies, and Raveis 1985, p. 73). Moreover, having multiple roles "increases opportunity for satisfaction" (Hammond 1988, p. 17).

> Multiple roles also provide legitimate excuses for failing to meet normal obligations; the competing demands of other roles may be cited. [And] multiple roles buffer the actor against the consequences of role failure or role loss. The actor has other involvements upon which to fall back (Thoits 1983, p. 184).

"Women with multiple roles end up with more duties, time pressures, and stresses[, increasing] their risks of acute and chronic health problems and [decreasing] their ability to spend time on health problems" (Verbrugge 1983, p. 16). But while women have more symptoms, men actually have poorer overall health.

Full-time employed people are much healthier than others. They have better self-rated health, fewer daily symptoms and chronic conditions, notably fewer restricted-activity days, fewer job limitations, less medical care, less curative drug use, and less prescription use (Verbrugge 1983, p. 21).

Apparently, multiple roles add focus and definition to life (Thoits 1983, p. 175). If a person has too many roles, however, overload, burnout, and strain are usually the results.

On the positive side, "employment and marriage are related to good physical health" (Verbrugge 1983, p. 16), and "people with the fewest family roles (nonmarried nonparents) have the poorest health profile" (p. 23). For men faculty, being married and having a family are factors that indicate maturity and a well-rounded personality. As noted earlier, however, women faculty are not so fortunate, because they typically have to make choices if they want to succeed in higher education. While one researcher found that "the combination of job and family roles has no special effect, positive or negative, on health" (Verbrugge 1983, p. 25), the addition of multiple roles typically creates distress. Fortunately, even though women experience higher levels of distress than men, as they age, achieve higher levels of education, and earn higher salaries, their levels of distress decrease (Thoits 1983).

On the contrary, perhaps working women have "less robust mental health than men not simply because they take on an additional number of tasks at home but more importantly because they are overwhelmed by the incessant demands of their children, which they constantly try to meet" (Sekaran 1986, p. 29). Their level of stress is also increased because they cannot make a complete commitment to their work or their careers (Sekaran 1986). Perhaps improved mental health occurs only for women whose husbands help with the work created by the family (Baruch, Biener, and Barnett 1987).

Given the fact that women in the same work situations could experience different stressors (Burke 1987), it is not surprising that their reactions to extreme distress are typically misunderstood. A study of 58 matched pairs of men and women faculty found that "female . . . faculty report more anxiety, stress, loneliness, and recurrent physical illness" than men faculty (Thoreson et al. 1990, p. 204), but this finding could be accounted for by the fact that women might be more aware of internal stressors, might be more inclined to disclose their feelings, or might actually experience more stress.

Summary
The literature both supports and refutes the claim that gender affects faculty members' job satisfaction; on balance, however, it appears that job satisfaction for women faculty is less than for men faculty. Apparently, some factors in the academic environment are not conducive to maximum productivity or to job satisfaction for women. It appears that women have heavier teaching and advising loads, which leads to insufficient time for research and to considerable strain. This inclination toward teaching for women also has a direct, negative effect on the receipt of rewards, such as salary, academic rank, and tenure.

Women faculty make lower salaries than their male colleagues, are typically not tenured, are clustered in the lowest academic ranks, can be found primarily in part-time positions, are employed in typically "feminine" disciplines, and are not usually employed at the most prestigious research-oriented institutions. Moreover, they believe that their superiors or colleagues do not value their input, and they are, more often than not, excluded from professional, male-oriented networks. In addition, women faculty believe they have no control over their working conditions, although they usually fare better when they work in institutions that are less highly dominated by men. Women faculty also believe they have to prove themselves over and over again before their colleagues can accept them and before they can achieve appropriate recognition. Perhaps this tiresome job of continually having to reaffirm their competence leads them frequently to question their qualifications and abilities to get the job done. It *is* possible that issues other than gender contribute to women faculty members' inability to attain equal status with men in the academy; on this point, additional research needs to be conducted.

Undeniably, marriage, parenting, caring for elderly parents, and domestic responsibilities create major obstacles to productivity for women faculty (Benton 1986; Crawford 1982; Villadsen and Tack 1981). Some women "view the joint commitment to the roles of wife and mother and professional career woman as a barrier [that] will prevent women from moving into and through the occupational world as equals with men" (Amatea and Cross 1981, p. 5).

Ideally the women at the university should represent a variety of life-styles, just as the male faculty members do. Some should be dedicated, and probably single, scholar-teachers, and others should be women who manage successfully to cope with the demands of academic life and of home and family (Graham 1971, p. 732).

Clearly, neither women nor men should have to choose between family and career but should be encouraged to have both, if they wish (Hensel 1991).

Overall, "both male and female faculty [report] similarly high levels of satisfaction with their personal and professional life . . . and overall satisfaction with [the] academic role" (Thoreson et al. 1990, p. 207). Because the challenge of balancing work and family responsibilities is so overwhelming, however, many married women, including women faculty, compromise their lives by diluting their professional ambitions and assuming part-time faculty positions or by working at a "teaching" rather than a "research" institution. Single women faculty also frequently forfeit marriage and families to achieve their goals. Regardless, such sacrifices are unjust and unnecessary.

Leaders in higher education must respond to the changes in society and the work force that have affected women faculty members' lives.

Although there is no clear evidence, some administrators— in industry even more than in academia—believe that addressing the changing needs of individuals and their families will yield advantages in recruitment, retention, productivity, and morale. If so, institutions of higher education need to assume a role in helping junior—as well as other [— faculty to] accommodate the competing demands of their careers and personal lives (Sorcinelli and Near 1989, p. 78).

Higher education officials should now be striving to develop rewards for women that will ensure greater job satis-

Leaders in higher education must respond to the changes in society and the work force that have affected women faculty members' lives.

faction for them and, subsequently, greater productivity. The small number of women who are associate and full professors reflects the serious lack of progress women have made in the academy (Gappa and Uehling 1979). Clearly, higher education cannot afford to allow women, who represent such a large, relatively untapped resource for the academy, to work at less than peak performance, to be dissatisfied with any aspect of their work lives, or to be stressed to the limit because of numerous life-style stressors. Moreover, given the fact that "the proportion of women doctorates who teach declined from 53 percent to 42 percent during . . . 1977 [to 1988]" ("Ph.D.s for Women Up" 1990, p. 4), immediate action must be taken to make a career in higher education more attractive to women with doctorates. Unquestionably, then, strategies for enhancing job satisfaction as a means of improving the recruitment and retention of women faculty, for making the faculty position a more attractive career option for females, and for eliminating dissatisfying factors in one's job need to be developed and implemented if equity in the workplace is in fact to become a reality.

While women's overall status in the faculty ranks has changed relatively little over the past two decades, more women are in faculty positions and involved in research and publication (Astin and Snyder 1982).

Academic men and women today are treated more nearly on a par. Women are better represented on campus. Even though there are still discrepancies in rank and salary, the gap has diminished considerably. There is a better balance between teaching and research for both men and women. Women engage in research and publication to a greater extent now than they did in the early 1970s (Astin and Snyder 1982, p. 31).

Perhaps a glimmer of hope exists that some day women will be able to achieve all they are capable of achieving in the academic environment.

MINORITY FACULTY

Without a doubt, the small number of minority faculty in higher education has become an important national issue. During academic year 1987–88, of the 489,000 full-time, regular instructional faculty in institutions of higher education, 21,000 were Asian, 16,000 were African-American, non-Hispanic, 11,000 were Hispanic, and 4,000 were American Indian (U.S. Dept. of Education 1991). The percentage for Asian-American, Mexican-American, Puerto Rican, and Hispanic faculty has increased in the relatively recent past. From 1975 to 1984, for instance, the percentage of Asian males in higher education increased from 2.2 to 3.1, the percentage of Asian females from 1.4 to 1.5 (Andersen, Carter, and Malizio 1989). During the same time, the total percentage of male and female faculty who were Mexican-American, Puerto Rican, and Hispanic increased from 0.4 to 1.2 (males) and 0.1 to 1.1 (females) (Andersen, Carter, and Malizio 1989). For American Indian and African-American faculty, however, the percentages declined—from 0.1 to 0 for American Indian males, from 0.2 to 0 for American Indian females, from 2.5 to 1.8 for African-American males, and from 4.6 to 3.6 for African-American females (Andersen, Carter, and Malizio 1989).

When armed with supporting information, institutional officials can often create an environment in which change can flourish, and the success of minority faculty can be the outcome. Consequently, this section focuses on the factors that affect the job satisfaction of minority faculty, specifically, the status of minorities in the faculty ranks and the need for increasing their numbers. Moreover, it provides information about the attitudes and perceptions of minority faculty regarding their satisfaction with salary, promotion and tenure, the work environment and working relationships, and racial climate. Unfortunately, research and writing about minority faculty other than African-Americans are lacking, making it necessary to use examples about African-Americans to emphasize certain points.

The Need for and Status of Minority Faculty

Minority faculty members are crucial to the personal and academic success of minority students. African-American students, who have decried the absence of African-American professionals in all roles on white campuses (Astin 1982; Burrell 1980; Jones 1979), need to see African-Americans in faculty positions, serving as role models and spokespeople for their race (Smith et al. 1986). "The absence of adequate black role models that function in both traditional and nontraditional roles tends to place great stress on black students" (p. 56). African-American faculty members can encourage students' professional growth and steer students toward career advancement (Smith et al. 1986). And they can assist African-American students in adjusting to white campuses, where they are often isolated or alienated (Vontress 1971) and experience some hostility from whites. Some African-American students feel more comfortable speaking to African-American faculty about personal problems and academic concerns because their cultural and social backgrounds or ideologies are the same. Likewise, Hispanic, Asian, and Native American students need faculty of their ethnic background to serve as role models, advisers, and mentors.

Minority faculty, especially at predominantly white institutions, can encourage minority students to achieve and maintain a sense of dignity. "Institutions of higher learning generally lack an environment that reinforces a sense of dignity for black students" (Smith et al. 1986, p. 55). Furthermore, more African-American faculty members are needed in higher education, because African-American students believe that the absence of African-American faculty parallels their own low status on campus (Smith and Zorn 1981). And it is likely that the experiences of students and faculty from other minority groups are similar.

The presence or absence of minority faculty members in graduate and professional schools is a good informal indicator of an institution's overall commitment to equal opportunity for minorities in higher education. If an institution cannot recruit, employ, and tenure a critical mass of minority faculty members, it is not likely that the same institution will be successful in recruiting, retaining, and graduating a significant number of minority students at any level (Epps 1989, p. 24).

The graduate experience for African-American students underscores the importance of mentors.

This training is accomplished most often through mentor relationships with professors; that is, students link up with faculty members through research and teaching assistant-

*ships and learn the "tricks of the trade." The professor thus
becomes a "role model" for the student. Moreover, a mentor
can smooth out bumps and rough spots on the graduate
journey, thus facilitating a student's passage through and
eventual graduation from graduate or professional school.
Unfortunately, many black students do not have the opportunity to experience such a relationship. . . . As a consequence, blacks are denied a valuable source of financial
support, practical experience in research and teaching, and
socioemotional support. . . . The final result? More black
students drop out, either terminating their studies with inter-
mediary degrees (e.g., M.A.s rather than Ph.D.s) or simply
leaving with no degree* (Hall and Allen 1983, p. 57).*

Another consequence of employing only a few minority
faculty members is the lack of opportunity for white students
to interact with minority faculty members. Clearly, taking a
course with a minority instructor is the best way for white students to overcome their prejudiced misconceptions about
the intellectual capabilities of minorities. To the degree that
experience is the best teacher, no substitute exists for interaction of this kind.* Finally, the low number of minority faculty decreases the chances for interaction among minority
and white faculty. Such communication allows white faculty
to gain a better understanding of minority cultures and fosters
collegiality.*

Minority academicians should be involved in research and
development for several critical reasons (Frierson 1990).

*Black [and other minority] faculty members bring a per-
spective based on their experiences and backgrounds that
makes for a more heterogeneous campus. Their presence
effectively serves to debunk the myth that scholarship and
academic excellence are the sole province of white faculty*
(Harvey and Scott-Jones 1985, p. 70).

In addition, minority faculty can serve as role models in the
research arena for their minority colleagues, proving that
minority faculty can be good scholars in higher education.
And through their research, minority faculty can identify variables that affect the recruitment, retention, and graduation

---

*W. Harvey 1989, personal communication.

of minority students and could cause institutional officials to review and revise policies and procedures.

As never before, more involvement and more black educational researchers are needed in the efforts to address the myriad problems that beset U.S. education. . . . The implications of educational research are wide ranging, for studies conducted by educational researchers can affect all forms of education relative to blacks and other Americans, and thus there is a need for more involvement of black educational researchers (Frierson 1990, p. 12).

Attitudes and Perceptions of Minority Faculty About Job Satisfaction

The topic of job satisfaction for minority faculty has gained some momentum recently. Three studies since 1988 involving large numbers of African-American respondents have focused on the topic (Logan 1990, with an *N* of 273, or 77 percent of those surveyed; Office of Instructional Research 1990, with an *N* of 413, or 39 percent of those surveyed; Silver, Dennis, and Spikes 1988, with an *N* of 523, or 55.2 percent of African-American faculty members surveyed). Because much of the information in this section comes from these three studies, information about the research methodologies used is also included.

Logan's study sought to determine the level of job satisfaction of African-American faculty at 28 four-year, state-assisted predominantly African-American and predominantly white institutions in the Southern Association of Colleges and Schools accreditation region. She mailed a demographic questionnaire, the Job in General scale, and the Job Descriptive Index to 355 African-American subjects. Of the 1,987 African-American faculty at the 13 predominantly African-American institutions, 208 received the surveys, and all 147 African-American faculty members at the 15 predominantly white institutions were invited to participate. Of the 355 instruments distributed, 273 were returned. For African-American faculty at the predominantly white institutions, 125, or 85 percent of the instruments, were returned; for African-American faculty at the predominantly African-American institutions, 148, or 71 percent of the instruments, were returned.

In the 1990 study of African-American faculty and administrators in the commonwealth of Virginia, 413, or 39 percent, of the 1,054 participants returned the Black Instructional Faculty and Administrators Satisfaction Survey. The purpose of the study was to assess the subjects' satisfaction with such variables as retention and recruitment, affirmative action, promotion and tenure, and the environment that existed in the community and city. Faculty and administrators at doctoral-degree-granting four-year traditionally black institutions, four-year traditionally white institutions, and community colleges were included in the study.

The third study, commissioned by the Southern Education Foundation (Silver, Dennis, and Spikes 1988), used the Questionnaire for Faculty of Public Higher Education Institutions to study characteristics, experiences, and perceptions of African-American faculty in traditionally white institutions in selected states. Of the 948 eligible African-American faculty, 55 percent responded; however, only 474, or 50 percent, of the respondents identified their ethnicity as "black." Therefore, the analyses in the report were based on the response of the group of 474 respondents.

By reviewing the research findings from these three studies and others that have focused on the job satisfaction of minority faculty, one can begin to understand the challenges faced by minority faculty members in U.S. higher education. To comprehend the magnitude of the problems that exist, it is important to understand the issues associated with overall job satisfaction as well as satisfaction with factors like salary, promotion and tenure, the work environment, and racial climate.

Overall Job Satisfaction

Historically, faculty members across the country have espoused feelings of good will and enthusiasm toward their work (Willie and Stecklein 1982). Nearly 82 percent of all instructional faculty at four-year, public, comprehensive institutions were satisfied with their jobs overall (American Association of State 1990). But regarding job satisfaction:

> . . . it appears that as a group, black faculty are less satisfied with their college/university positions than are white faculty. . . . Black faculty, relative to whites, perceive themselves to be less respected, to receive less satisfaction from their positions, and to have less certain employment futures (Davis 1985, p. 90).

These conclusions come from a study limited to African-American faculty in social work departments; however, the following perceptions developed before the study on African-American faculty at traditionally white institutions were found to be true:

1. In the areas of salary, promotion, and tenure, a significant portion of African-American faculty members perceive they are unfairly treated.
2. With respect to salary and advancement, African-American faculty members perceive more inequity than do whites.
3. African-American faculty members are generally not satisfied with their work environment.
4. African-Americans do not perceive that they are in the professional mainstream at their institutions.
5. As a result of relatively recent entry into the academy, African-American faculty members hold a different view about the factor important to career advancement than do white faculty members (Silver, Dennis, and Spikes 1988, p. 13).

Salary

Salary is an essential career barometer for faculty (Silver, Dennis, and Spikes 1988) and affects the level of teachers' morale (Rempel and Bentley 1970). Further, the "perceived inequities in wages and salaries tend to contribute more to work dissatisfaction than the exact amount of pay" (Ivancevich and Donnelly 1968, p. 176), and the highest level of job dissatisfaction is with the appropriateness of the participants' salary (Silver, Dennis, and Spikes 1988). As shown in table 3, 41.5 percent of the respondents either "strongly disagreed" or "disagreed with reservations" that their salary was appropriate for their rank and experience.

Not surprisingly, many predominantly white colleges have sought and attracted the best-educated African-American scholars with salaries that are superior to those offered at predominantly African-American institutions (Moore and Wagstaff 1974), thus creating major personnel problems for the African-American colleges. "It is widely acknowledged that most black schools suffer from serious shortages of funds and employ underpaid faculties . . . " (Fleming 1984, p. 15). In the struggle to keep tuition competitive, funds available for faculty at

TABLE 3

BLACK FACULTY ATTITUDES AND PERCEPTIONS ABOUT
SALARY, TENURE, AND PROMOTION

Item	Strongly Disagree	Disagree with Reservations	Agree with Reservations	Strongly Agree	N
Salary is appropriate for rank and experience	23.0	18.5	37.7	20.8	443
Compared to colleagues, research rewarded equitably	14.0	20.8	38.6	26.6	394
Compared to colleagues, teaching rewarded equitably	13.6	18.1	39.4	28.9	426
Promotion and tenure procedures equitable	12.8	23.9	43.1	20.3	439
Tenure status appropriate	15.9	11.3	31.4	41.3	433
Student evaluations fair and equitable	8.2	11.2	37.6	43.0	428
Supervisor evaluations fair and equitable	7.0	9.3	40.7	43.0	440

Source: Silver, Dennis, and Spikes 1988, p. 77, table 37.

African-American colleges are at a minimal level (Bowles and Decosta 1971; Jones and Weathersby 1978).

> *The salary structure in most black colleges is noncompetitive with white colleges, even within the same state and often within the same system of higher education. . . . It is difficult to find a black college in the nation that pays competitive faculty salaries with its white counterparts* (Billingsley 1982, p. 10).

Logan, however, found no significant difference in the level of satisfaction with salary for African-American faculty at predominantly African-American or at predominantly white institutions. The salaries of faculty at the predominantly African-American institutions were competitive with the salaries of faculty at predominantly white institutions. Specifically, 49 percent of the respondents earned $25,000 to $34,999, 6.9 percent were paid $45,000 or more, and only 7.8 percent earned $19,999 or less. The average salary for African-American faculty at predominantly African-American institutions was $33,520, the average salary for those at predominantly white institutions $32,335. Further, the salary faculty received affected their satisfaction with present pay (Logan 1990). With the exception of those earning $29,999 or less, African-American faculty with higher salaries reported higher levels of job satisfaction.

In the study in Virginia, "approximately 70 percent of all respondents perceive both their initial and current salaries as somewhat commensurate with their experience and duties, although women felt less satisfaction with their initial salaries than did men" (Office of Instructional Research 1990, p. 7). When African-American faculty and administrators were asked whether they agreed that there were "inequities in salary" or whether they thought salary inequities existed at their institution, the overall mean was 1.64, using a scale of $0 =$ not at all and $3 =$ very much. Interestingly, faculty perceived less inequity in salaries than administrators.

In terms of salary differentials for faculty representing different ethnic minority groups, no comparative statistics surfaced in the literature. This void is not surprising, as African-Americans were the predominant minority group involved in higher education until the beginning of the last decade.

Promotion and tenure

Promotion and tenure are also excellent indicators of success for faculty (Silver, Dennis, and Spikes 1988), and low job satisfaction is frequently associated with limited opportunities for advancement through the ranks (Bureau of Institutional Research 1974). "The tenure rates of minority faculty continue to be lower than [those] of whites" ("Minorities in Higher Education" 1992, p. 10). Of all groups, including American Indians and Asian-Americans, African-Americans are the least likely to be tenured (Maxwell 1981). Further, whites are twice as likely as African-Americans to be tenured (Moore and Wagstaff 1974; Rafky 1972). In 1988, only 46 percent of African-American faculty at public four-year, comprehensive institutions had earned tenure, compared to approximately 88 percent of white, Hispanic, and Asian faculty at the same types of institutions (American Association of State 1990).

In the "up to 5 years" category, 89.6 percent of the black faculty have not been tenured; in the "5 to 10 years" category, 75.9 percent have not been tenured; in the "10 to 15 years" category, 49 percent have not been tenured; and in the "15 or more years" category, 49.1 percent have not been tenured. If there is a direct correlation between tenure and job satisfaction, most of the black . . . faculty . . . possessed little or no job security (Silver, Dennis, and Spikes 1988, pp. 44, 51).

In addition, more than one-quarter of the African-Americans in one study believed that African-Americans had to have better credentials than whites to be hired and granted tenure at an institution (Rafky 1972). Accordingly, promotion and tenure appear to be a "no-no" for African-American faculty (Moore and Wagstaff 1974). As one Ph.D. respondent stated, "Black professors with faculty status seem to be part of a cycling process. A maximum (quota) is maintained but no one stays the required five years, earliest date for tenure" (Moore and Wagstaff 1974, pp. 136–37). Further:

... only 46 percent of African-American faculty at public four-year, comprehensive institutions had earned tenure, compared to approximately 88 percent of white. . . .

> *Many departments have never hired more than a single black person. In several instances, those blacks have become victimized by the* revolving door *syndrome. That is to say, they perform services to an institution, a department, or some other academic unit for a probationary period. At the end of that period, a decision is reached that said person has not met the requirements for permanence of position and is dismissed. That person is replaced by another black who goes through the identical process. Consequently, few blacks are ever awarded tenure in predominantly white institutions* (Blackwell 1983, pp. 67–68).

At predominantly African-American institutions, however, African-American faculty members are more likely to be tenured. For example, 64.3 percent of the African-American faculty in one study were tenured at the predominantly African-American institutions, whereas only 29.3 percent were tenured at the predominantly white institutions (Logan 1990).

The greatest percentage of African-American faculty members on predominantly white campuses held the rank of assistant professor and, of the respondents initially hired at that rank, 64.3 percent said they had not been promoted (Silver, Dennis, and Spikes 1988). Even in the historically black colleges, both private and public, "Asian-Americans and whites were more likely to be employed as professors . . . and associate professors . . . than were blacks" (National

Advisory Committee 1980, p. 24). African-Americans were also underrepresented as assistant professors and constituted a larger proportion than whites or Asian-Americans only at the rank of instructor.

During fall 1985, of all African-American, non-Hispanic faculty members, most (31 percent) were assistant professors, 22 percent were associate professors, and 15 percent were full professors (U.S. Dept. of Education 1991). Interestingly, 28 percent of the total faculty were full professors, indicating a 13 percent discrepancy as far as African-Americans are concerned (see table 4). Further, most African-American faculty members in Logan's study were assistant professors (i.e., 33 percent were assistant professors at the predominantly African-American institutions and nearly 53 percent were assistant professors at the predominantly white institutions), a finding that is consistent with earlier results (Silver, Dennis, and Spikes 1988). When compared with the percentage (31 percent) of full-time African-American, non-Hispanic instructional faculty who were assistant professors in institutions of higher education (as reported by the U.S. Dept. of Education [1991]), the percentage of African-American faculty who were assistant professors at the predominantly white institutions (53 percent) in Logan's study was much higher.

TABLE 4

FULL-TIME INSTRUCTIONAL FACULTY IN INSTITUTIONS OF HIGHER EDUCATION BY ACADEMIC RANK (Fall 1985)

Academic Rank	Total Number of Faculty Members	Percent of Total	African-American Non-Hispanic	Percent of Total	Percent Difference
Men and women, all ranks	464,072		19,227		
Professors	129,269	27.9	2,859	14.9	–13.0
Associate professors	111,092	23.9	4,201	21.8	–2.1
Assistant professors	111,308	24.0	5,895	30.7	6.7
Instructors	75,411	16.2	4,572	23.8	7.6
Lecturers	9,766	2.1	631	3.3	1.2
Other faculty	27,226	5.9	1,069	5.5	–0.4

Source: U.S. Dept. of Education 1991, p. 219, table 212.

Like African-Americans, "members of other minorities, and white women, Hispanics are concentrated at the lower levels of academic employment. They are more likely to be instructors rather than assistant, associate, or full professors" (Nieves-Squires 1991, p. 2) (see table 5).

TABLE 5

HISPANIC FACULTY MEMBERS IN COLLEGES AND UNIVERSITIES AS A PERCENTAGE OF ALL FACULTY MEMBERS

Rank	Women	Men
Professor	0.2%	0.9%
Associate professor	0.4%	1.2%
Assistant professor	0.6%	1.2%
Instructor/lecturer	0.9%	1.4%

Source: Nieves-Squires 1991; Wilson and Carter 1988.

When compared with other minority groups, American Indian faculty members have fared similarly ("Minorities in Higher Education" 1992). As for Asian-American faculty members, however, the situation is much more positive:

In the aggregate, the promotion and tenure rates for Asian-Americans are lower than the national average but higher than for other comparable minority groups. Further, those Asian-Americans that enter academe are promoted and tenured at higher rates and in less time than all comparable faculty groups (Brown 1988, p. 27).

Interestingly, faculty at predominantly white institutions were more satisfied with opportunities for promotion than their counterparts at predominantly African-American institutions, and tenured faculty at the predominantly African-American institutions and nontenured faculty at the predominantly white institutions were more satisfied with opportunities for promotion than were the nontenured faculty at the predominantly African-American institutions (Logan 1990). Another, earlier study found no significant differences in faculty satisfaction with opportunities for promotion between tenured and nontenured groups (Sprague 1974). In addition, men reported more satisfaction with opportunities for promotion than did women (Logan 1990). And opportunities for promotion differed significantly by rank between professors and associate professors, compared to instructors, with instructors reporting the lowest satisfaction and professors the highest (Logan 1990).

As indicated earlier, achieving the rank of full professor has been difficult for minority faculty who hold lower rank at predominantly white institutions. In a study conducted in New York, New Jersey, and Connecticut to identify impediments to hiring, promotion, and tenure in predominantly white colleges and universities, African-American and Hispanic faculty cited lack of publications as the major factor in the denial of tenure for minority professionals (National Urban League 1982). Further, "the reward system of promoting academics on the grounds of research and published scholarship has become more deeply rooted in the universities, and would-be universities and leading four-year colleges, with every passing decade" (Clark 1989, p. 5). Besides being denied tenure for lack of publications, minority professionals:

> *Do not think that community service and counseling to minority students are given sufficient consideration in the tenure and promotion review. Half of the professionals indicated that minority community activities were not positively evaluated at their institutions, and nearly half (47 percent) of the sample felt that advisement to minority students was not positively evaluated* (National Urban League 1982, p. xii).

Additionally, "most respondents (73.7 percent) [in the Virginia study of African-American faculty and administrators] report that involvement with black student groups and similar activities plays little or no significant part in tenure and/or promotion decisions . . . (Office of Instructional Research 1990, p. 5).

In other words, becoming involved in the advising of minority students and maintaining relationships with members of the minority community might not be viewed positively in the decision to award tenure. Although advising students might not assist white faculty either in the decision to award tenure, African-American faculty members must deal with inordinately heavy roles as student advisers and spokespeople (Frierson 1990; Staples 1984); " . . . some departments 'direct anything black' toward the lone black faculty member" (Blackwell 1983, p. 68). The same situation holds true for Hispanic faculty:

Sometimes there is a tacit assumption that all Hispanic students should be advised by the sole or few Hispanic faculty members, even though the numbers may outstrip those assigned to other faculty members. In addition to those students formally assigned, a number of others may gravitate to Hispanic faculty members to seek informal guidance (Nieves-Squires 1991, p. 5).

In the future, minority faculty must be given credit in promotion and tenure equations for advising minority students and acting as spokespeople for minorities. The needs of minority students and the numerous work-related assignments minority faculty are now expected to complete must become part of the review before promotion and awarding tenure. Otherwise, institutions cannot ask minority faculty to continue their current level of mentoring, role modeling, and representation (Black 1981).

The work environment
"Faculty tend to derive satisfaction from the nature of their work itself, while they tend to express dissatisfaction most frequently with extrinsic factors, such as salary [and] administrative leadership . . . " (Finkelstein 1978, p. 229). Some of the important internal dimensions of their work are autonomy and freedom (Eckert and Stecklein 1961; French, Tupper, and Mueller 1965; Gustad 1960; Moses 1986; Pelz and Andrews 1976), intellectual interchange (Eckert and Stecklein 1961; Gustad 1960), student-teacher interaction and students' learning (Bess 1981; Cohen 1973, 1974; Eckert and Stecklein 1961; Wilson, Woods, and Gaff 1974; Winkler 1982), and responsibility (Herzberg 1972; Herzberg, Mausner, and Snyderman 1959). Other important factors in the workplace include working relationships, identification with the department and the institution, and appointment or election to committees (Silver, Dennis, and Spikes 1988).

As shown in table 6, 42 percent of respondents either "agreed with reservations" or "strongly agreed" that it is difficult to be appointed to important committees, and over half

(51 percent) either "agreed with reservations" or "strongly agreed" that it is difficult to be elected to important committees (Silver, Dennis, and Spikes 1988, p. 81). Similarly, minority professionals do not generally serve on the committees that would increase their chances for promotion and tenure (National Urban League 1982); specifically, between 1978 and 1981, only half of the respondents in the Tri-State Minority Faculty study had served on hiring, promotion, and tenure committees. Although "committees [that] shaped academic policy were very important in assisting mobility, 56 percent indicated that their chances for appointments to those committees were poor or that they had no chance at all in comparison to whites" (National Urban League 1982, p. xii). More-

TABLE 6

BLACK FACULTY MEMBERS' ATTITUDES AND PERCEPTIONS ABOUT THE WORK ENVIRONMENT

Item	Strongly Disagree	Disagree with Reservations	Agree with Reservations	Strongly Agree	N
Professional ambition achievable at present institution	18.4	18.2	35.3	28.1	456
Good working relationships easily developed in department	9.9	17.7	37.1	35.2	463
Good working relationships easily developed in institution	10.2	29.5	45.1	15.2	461
Skills and experiences could be better used	9.1	17.8	34.7	38.4	450
Input in departmental matters well received	8.3	15.5	39.6	36.5	457
Have real sense of identification with department	11.3	17.4	36.2	35.1	459
Have real sense of identification with institution	13.9	25.7	41.6	18.7	459
Have had opportunities to serve on important committees	10.4	13.2	32.1	44.3	461
Difficult to be appointed to important committees	25.2	33.4	25.9	15.9	452
Difficult to be elected to important committees	19.5	29.6	31.6	19.3	446

Source: Silver, Dennis, and Spikes 1988, p. 81, table 39.

over, while the same situation is likely true for faculty members from other minority groups, "Hispanic participation in university committees is often related to ethnic factors" (Washington and Harvey 1989, p. 27). "Committees concerned with larger campus, instructional, research, and related policy issues are rarely among the list of choices available to Hispanic faculty" (Garza 1988, p. 124)—and presumably other minority faculty as well.

In contrast, minorities perceive their chances as being better than those of whites for service on committees that make decisions about affirmative action and student affairs. Only one-fourth of the professionals, however, thought that service on affirmative action committees assisted them in achieving promotion and tenure (National Urban League 1982, pp. xii–xiii).

Concerning relationships in the work environment, one reason African-Americans leave predominantly white institutions, where they frequently find themselves small in numbers and isolated (Andrulis, Sikes, and Friedman 1975), relates to their desire to work for and with other African-Americans (Moore and Wagstaff 1974). Because of the larger number of African-American students at predominantly African-American institutions, "many highly talented black faculty members regularly refuse offers to go to white colleges precisely because they feel the greatest challenge in higher education is the education of black youth and the building of strong black faculties" (Billingsley 1982, p. 11). In the Tri-State study, the greatest source of job dissatisfaction (43 percent) was the lack of opportunity for association with other minority professionals. In another study, 68 percent of the African-American faculty agreed with the statement that "I need contact with other black faculty and black students to make my job environment more satisfying" (Elmore and Blackburn 1983), p. 12). Moreover, "the percentage of black faculty and staff employed and the number of black students enrolled [were not factors] in accepting the current position for 67.8 percent of the respondents . . . " (Office of Instructional Research 1990, p. 6). "Psychologically, black faculty often find themselves in work environments that are not fully supportive. Prejudice and discrimination remain as obstacles, and for many the lack of mentoring, at any level, is a reality" (Frierson 1990, p. 12).

Because of the larger number of minorities in predominantly African-American institutions, faculty could feel more content with their working relationships and have a stronger sense of identity. But in a recent study of African-American faculty at traditionally white institutions, 72 percent agreed that good working relationships are easily developed in the department, and 60 percent believed that such relationships are easily developed in the institution (Silver, Dennis, and Spikes 1988).

Nontenured African-American faculty at predominantly white institutions were more satisfied with their co-workers than were nontenured African-American faculty members at predominantly African-American institutions (Logan 1990). (It must not be assumed that the nontenured African-Americans at the predominantly African-American institutions were working only with co-workers of their ethnicity.) Further, tenured faculty at the predominantly African-American institutions were more satisfied with their co-workers than were their nontenured counterparts, supporting the conclusion that nontenured faculty are significantly less satisfied than tenured faculty (Sprague 1974).

Moreover, African-American faculty at predominantly white institutions were more satisfied with their supervision than were African-American faculty members at predominantly African-American institutions (Logan 1990). Again, one must not assume that the faculty person was or was not satisfied with a supervisor of his or her same ethnicity. In fact, the chair was sometimes white, not African-American. As one respondent noted, "Often . . . the balance of 'power' is not with blacks within the predominantly black institutions" (Logan 1990, p. 110).

Racial climate
Organizational climate affects job satisfaction (Sprague 1974) in that a positive environment frequently relates to high motivation, job satisfaction, and improved work performance (Hellriegel and Slocum 1974; LaFollette and Sims 1975; Litwin and Stringer 1968). Certainly, few, if any, minority faculty members will be content at an institution where a climate of racism lingers; consequently, an organizational culture that supports racism is one factor that contributes to the dissatisfaction, and the ultimately declining numbers, of African-American faculty at predominantly white institutions. While overt racial discrimination might not exist:

In the majority of situations, when there is a faculty position to be filled, the decision about who is hired to occupy a vacant slot is largely made by the people who already hold faculty status. Overwhelmingly, those people are likely to be white and male, and available data clearly show that the person chosen is most likely to be a white male. . . . The excuses offered for not hiring blacks for faculty positions range from their having a less impressive background than the white candidate to their not being a "good fit" with the rest of the faculty. *

African-American faculty who reported about their perceptions of the racial climate at predominantly white institutions (see table 7) "agreed with reservations" or "strongly agreed" that their institutions were committed to improvement in minority affairs (52 percent) but also disagreed with all other statements about racial climate (Silver, Dennis, and Spikes 1988). In addition, 75 percent "disagreed with reservations" or "strongly disagreed" that minority faculty membership was sufficient on faculty search committees, and over 79 percent "disagreed with reservations" or "strongly disagreed" that minority faculty representation was sufficient in their departments. And 91 percent "disagreed with reserva-

*W. Harvey 1989, personal communication.

TABLE 7

BLACK FACULTY MEMBERS' ATTITUDES AND PERCEPTIONS ABOUT RACIAL CLIMATE

Item	Strongly Disagree	Disagree with Reservations	Agree with Reservations	Strongly Agree	N
Institution is committed to improvement in minority affairs	21.8	26.6	39.9	11.8	459
Faculty search committees have sufficient minority membership	41.5	33.4	20.1	5.0	443
Department has appropriate minority faculty representation	58.3	21.1	13.6	7.0	456
Institution has appropriate minority faculty representation	73.4	17.9	7.2	1.5	458
My ethnic background enhances my opportunity for advancement	36.6	38.0	20.1	5.1	453

Source: Silver, Dennis, and Spikes 1988, p. 90, table 43.

tions" or "strongly disagreed" that their institutions had appropriate minority faculty representation, while 75 percent "disagreed with reservations" or "strongly disagreed" that their ethnic background enhanced their opportunity for advancement.

In many cases when an African-American faculty member is employed at a predominantly white institution, he or she is not only the sole African-American person in the department, but also the only one in the college. "Many departments have never hired more than a single black person" (Blackwell 1983, p. 67), and "when there is only one or a very small number of black faculty members in a given institution, the burdens of institutional and individual racism weigh heavily" (Harvey and Scott-Jones 1985, p. 70). In such a situation, a person might not be psychologically supported, because understanding, warmth, and empathy are not always part of the environment.

> *In the absence of a support group operating under the same circumstances, frustrations understandably mount. Black faculty members are subjected to the aggravating aspects of the academic milieu without enjoying some of its compensating benefits: contemplation, independence, and social and intellectual stimulation from colleagues sharing the same interests and outlook* (Harvey and Scott-Jones 1985, p. 70).

Understandably, the scholarly productivity of African-American and other minority faculty (a primary criterion for promotion and tenure) could be negatively affected in a work environment where a hostile racial climate exists. Worse yet:

> *Black faculty may often receive messages that their work focusing on or addressing issues that affect minorities warrants little scholarly respect. As a consequence, some black faculty may feel pressured to compromise their research interests and to focus more on what their white colleagues may deem acceptable. Because of pressures to conform to values associated with mainstream research, they may thus find themselves in academic environments that, for them, are intellectually and professionally stifling* (Frierson 1990, p. 13).

The same situation affects other minority groups as well. "Hispanic faculty are often 'type cast' as specialists in ethnic matters rather than as 'qualified' in a particular discipline," a perception that has developed partly as a result of Hispanic faculty members' research interests (Washington and Harvey 1989, p. 27). Moreover:

Two out of every three Hispanic faculty in [social sciences, education, and humanities] wrote doctoral dissertations dealing with their own racial/ethnic group, Latin America, minorities, or other related topics. These research interests often provide an easy excuse for their being hired to teach in only a limited number of academic areas. However, while these research interests partially explain their concentration in a limited number of academic departments, it does not explain why Hispanic sociologists, historians, etc., are often perceived by non-Hispanic decision makers and other faculty members as being Latino, Chicano, Puerto Rican specialists, rather than real or full-fledged sociologists, historians, etc., in their own right (Garza 1988, p. 123).

Summary

If institutions of higher education expect to increase the number of minority faculty, members of the academy must know why dissatisfied minorities leave the profession, because their dissatisfactions in areas like salary, promotion, and tenure could be the reasons institutions are unable to retain them. All of the following factors influence turnover: organization-wide factors (policies regarding pay and promotion), the immediate work environment (unit size, supervision, and relationships with co-workers), job-related factors (nature of job requirements), and personal factors (age and tenure) (Porter and Steers 1973). Moreover, satisfaction with the organization and faculty members' "expressed intention to remain [in the work setting] were positively related to salary, length of time in the organization, and tenure" (Pfeffer and Lawler 1980, p. 38).

Besides low salaries and the difficulty of obtaining tenure and promotion, minority faculty can be hard to retain if they feel isolated and are unable to achieve success in a predominantly white environment. According to one African-American faculty member describing a year at a university in Maine, " . . . All the people were white. . . . My kids were harassed in school every day. During the entire year, no one invited me to dinner, or even for a drink . . . " (Wilson 1987, p. 14). This faculty member left the institution at the end of the year because of isolation in a hostile environment (Wilson 1987).

Discrimination could be a strong factor leading to the inability to retain minority faculty. In a study of African-American scholars, African-American professors explained why their African-American acquaintances who are qualified for the academic profession were attracted to other occupations (Rafky 1972). The largest percentage (33 percent) listed discrimination as the reason they chose other professions. Thus, some of the factors that have influenced African-American faculty to leave their universities relate to perceived racial discrimination and difficulty in obtaining promotion or tenure (Curry-Williams 1985). Other reasons for the declining number of African-American faculty in higher education include the failure or ineffectiveness of the affirmative action system, the decision to work in fields offering better opportunities (government, industry, foundations, and service agencies, for example [Rafky 1972]), and the "ripple effect" in terms of reduced numbers of African-American graduate students and persons available to fill future faculty positions (Harvey and Scott-Jones 1985; Wilson and Melendez 1985).

Unquestionably, minority faculty members are important to both minority and white students. The presence of minority faculty members allows white students the opportunity to interact with minority faculty as a means of overcoming their prejudiced misconceptions about the intellectual capabilities of minorities. Minority faculty provide support for minority colleagues. And the involvement of minority academicians in research and development is critical to both the advancement of knowledge and society's improvement.

The presence of minority faculty is essential to the maintenance of a culturally and ethnically diverse academic environment. "More than two-thirds of the nation's aging professoriate will have to be replaced by the end of the century" (Payne 1989, p. 22), but few minorities will likely be willing to assume faculty positions in higher education unless the rewards associated with the job change dramatically.

ISSUES AND STRATEGIES FOR RECRUITING AND RETAINING WOMEN AND MINORITY FACULTY

Even though nearly two decades have passed since the enactment of affirmative action laws in the United States, higher education remains largely a white male enterprise. In fact, "despite its rhetoric, and its attention to the undeniable force of changing demographics, the power of tradition and past practice in higher education militate against the diversity it so desperately seeks" (Sanders and Mellow 1990, p. 9).

Greater diversity is desirable [, however,] because the population of the nation is increasingly diverse, because problems and our approaches to them are complex and require the efforts of many kinds of expertise, and because a multicultural workplace is becoming the norm for all sectors of society, higher education included. Diversity is also demanded by the populations of students who enter our institutions, by the taxpayers who support, in one form or another, all of our institutions, and by the ideals of the nation as they have evolved over our history in law, precedent, and practice (Moore and Johnson 1989, p. 46).

Without the contribtions of minority individuals, no faculty or institution can be complete.

Unquestionably, as an industry, higher education must resolve a number of significant staffing issues if a cadre of women and minority faculty is to be available during the latter part of the 1990s and into the 21st century.

Faculty create the curriculum and determine the quality of the experience in every classroom. They serve as teachers, mentors, advisors, and role models. In a word, faculty are the core of the institution. Without the contributions of minority individuals, no faculty or institution can be complete (Green 1989, p. 81).

As is evident from the preceding sections, women and minority faculty are frequently dissatisfied with the personal and professional rewards associated with their jobs. Consequently, a position in the faculty is often not viewed as a viable career choice for young women and minorities, thus creating problems of supply and demand. As a result, it is imperative that special attention be paid to employing, and then enhancing job satisfaction for, the men and women who can bring multicultural and multiethnic perspectives to the academic environment.

A review of the literature available about strategies for identifying, recruiting, selecting, nurturing, and retaining minority and women faculty yields numerous conventional approaches that have been used repeatedly to increase the number of women and minority faculty in higher education: selecting and retaining a chief executive officer who is unmistakably committed to a diverse faculty, establishing and enforcing institutional and departmental affirmative action goals and timetables, ensuring the presence of women and minorities on all search committees, advertising positions in journals with minority and women readers, developing and/or using national data bases containing names of minority and women graduate students, fostering informal networking among minority and women faculty, sponsoring professional development conferences on issues of interest to minorities and women, engaging in faculty exchanges with historically black and women's colleges, and writing descriptions of positions so they will capture the interest of women and minority candidates. Implementing these strategies must be continued, but it is *mandatory* that they be supplemented with some nontraditional—perhaps even unconventional—methods.

Given the fact that a problem of crisis proportions now exists in terms of the availability of qualified minorities and women who can fill faculty positions in the future, fresh, extraordinary approaches must be identified. First, the issue of a lack of qualified individuals in the pipeline must be addressed for both the long term and the short term; logically, if a diverse faculty is to become a reality, a steady stream of minorities and women must be available in undergraduate and graduate schools who are preparing to assume faculty positions. Second, once women and minorities graduate, faculty positions must be attractive and represent viable career choices. Third, incentives and rewards must be available to department heads, deans, and faculty who are successful in their efforts to hire and support minorities and women for faculty positions.

Addressing the Problem of the Pipeline

Creating a cohort of qualified minorities and women to fill vacant faculty positions in postsecondary education will be a problem with which institutional leaders and senior faculty will have to deal for quite some time. Consequently, strategic or long-term plans must be developed to ensure that adequate numbers of individuals with appropriate credentials are available when they are needed. Over the next 40 to 50 years, it is possible for the supply of women and minorities interested in faculty positions to match the institutional demand for them, but the issue cannot be allowed to lie dormant for such an extended period of time. Both long-term and short-term mechanisms for providing a diverse faculty must also be identified and used immediately.

Long-term strategies

Increasing the number of women and minorities in the academic pipeline (Green 1989) is certainly one viable long-term strategy for solving the problem of diversity among college and university faculty. Existing faculty members and administrative personnel will need to develop sophisticated approaches to career planning that include a faculty position as a rational choice for students when they are making initial decisions about careers, perhaps even as early as junior high school. It is *never* too early to begin talking with young men and women about higher education as a viable choice of career. Moreover, "departments and individual faculty members should design summer and other programs that enable undergraduate students, including those recruited from other institutions (such as [historically black colleges and universities] and state university campuses with substantial populations of minority students), to participate in faculty research projects" (Justus, Freitag, and Parker 1987, p. 9). In 1981, for example, the University of Michigan initiated a program in scholarly research for urban and minority high school students; as part of that program, students participate in an active research relationship with a faculty member at the institution during their sophomore or junior high school years. Through such early contacts, institutional representatives will be able to acquaint young minorities with the benefits of a career in higher education.

Guarantees of financial support during their baccalaureate, master's, and doctoral studies must be given to prospective faculty members. Because most minorities and women have long-term financial responsibilities to their families, it is essential that funds be available to support them through receipt of their doctoral degrees. In other words, invitations to consider a career in higher education must be backed up with a commitment to assist talented young minorities and women in achieving the goals of earning a doctorate and being employed in a college or university.

> *The timing of awards of these sources of financial assistance [research and teaching assistantships] should be deliberately structured to provide maximum training. Thus, research assistantships . . . should be provided for the first two years; teacher assistantships . . . should be awarded after these two years, when a student has amassed enough information to perform well. . . . In addition, faculty should see their support of the final years of graduate work as similarly crucial. They need to assist graduate students to find fellowships to support the research and [writing] phases of the doctoral process* (Justus, Freitag, and Parker 1987, pp. 9–10.

One example of an attractive fellowship is the McKnight Doctoral Fellowship in arts and sciences, mathematics, business, and engineering offered through the Florida Endowment Fund for Higher Education.

> *The McKnight Doctoral Fellowship provides up to $5,000 in tuition and fees plus an annual stipend of $11,000 to 25 African-American citizens to pursue Ph.D. degrees at participating Florida universities. . . . Contingent upon successful academic progress, the maximum length of awards is four or five years, depending on the institution. The Florida Endowment Fund provides the first three years and the student's university continues funding at the same level of support for a fourth and in many cases a fifth year* ("Florida Endowment Fund" 1990, p. 12).

Others include, but are not limited to, the Richard F. Pride Research Fellowship at the University of South Florida, the Thurgood Marshall Dissertation Fellowships for African-American Scholars at Dartmouth College, the Minority Graduate Fellowships for Dissertation Research and Writing at George Washington University (*Black Issues in Higher Education* 1991), the Future Faculty Fellows Program at Temple University, and the State University of New York's Underrepresented Graduate Fellowship Program (*Black Issues in Higher Education* 1992).

Perhaps it is time for institutional officials to rethink the policy of not hiring their own graduates when minorities and women are involved (Boyd 1989). Institutions in the future that expect to have a diverse faculty might need to identify, educate, train, hire, and retain their own minority and women graduates. Through early identification, students can be encouraged to pursue their undergraduate and graduate studies at an institution and to culminate their education with employment in the faculty at their alma mater. By developing at the outset guarantees of employment for a specified period of time, the institution will be assured that the selected women and minorities will remain with the institution. Such an approach will provide mutual benefits: The institution will gain a minority or woman faculty member who has been trained to assume a faculty position, and the student will not have to worry about employment after graduation.

California State University at Bakersfield uses such a "grow-your-own" approach, "[identifying] ethnic minority individuals interested in pursuing a doctoral degree and [supporting] them financially up to a certain amount" (Arciniega 1990, p. 22).

Couple this with a loan forgiveness option, whereby an individual is provided with up to a maximum of $30,000 to complete his or her doctoral studies. Provided he or she agrees to return to . . . CSU to teach, the institution commits itself to employing the individual, as well as to providing the loan. Such loans can be completely forgiven if the individual returns to teach [at CSU] for five years. Should the individual choose to leave prior to that time, then he or she is obligated to pay the difference (Arciniega 1990, p. 22).

Short-term strategies
The problem with the pipeline will not be solved overnight; therefore, some consideration must be given to ways of recruiting women and minority immediately. For instance, in dealing with the lack of minority faculty, institutions can initiate faculty exchange programs with historically black institutions and colleges or universities that serve a Hispanic or women's population, perhaps the most effective short-term arrangement available (Justus, Freitag, and Parker 1987). While faculty exchange programs with historically black, Hispanic, or women's institutions will immediately put current students

in contact with minority and women faculty role models, it will also expand the institution's future base for recruitment by fostering contacts with minority and women faculty as well as higher education administrators who can refer prospective faculty.

On a statewide basis, for example, for a number of years and until 1992 (when severe financial difficulties surfaced), Michigan provided funds for the Martin Luther King, Jr.–Cesar Chavez–Rosa Parks Visiting Professor Program, which was designed to "increase the supply of minority instructors available to postsecondary education in Michigan" (Minority Resource Center 1990, p. 33). While the state no longer funds the positions, many of the institutions have allocated some of their scarce institutional funds to continue the program as an indication of their commitment to a diverse faculty. Moreover, "the [University of Michigan] currently is involved in more than a dozen collaborative efforts" with historically black colleges and universities and Hispanic institutions, "involving faculty exchanges, student transfer programs, and faculty collaborations" (Seidman 1990b, p. 1). Another successful program for visiting professors is the University of Kansas's Langston Hughes Visiting Professorship.

In addition, institutions can "create research jobs or part-time teaching positions for minority individuals . . . [and] postdoctoral fellowships as an enticement to minorities for permanent faculty positions" (Green 1989, pp. 84–85). Highly acclaimed postdoctoral fellowships for minorities and women are in place in the University of California, the University of North Carolina at Chapel Hill, and the University of Illinois at Urbana/Champaign (Green 1989). The University of Michigan's Visiting Professors Program, which began in 1986, demonstrates that success is possible. Since its beginnings:

The university's academic units have hosted over 100 distinguished scholars and professionals from across the United States. Visiting Professors represent ethnic groups traditionally underrepresented in postsecondary education: African-Americans, Asian-Americans, Hispanic Americans, and Native Americans. Representing a wide variety of academic disciplines, Visiting Professors present lectures and symposia, teach minicourses, give concerts, conduct standard-length courses, and exhibit their works of art. They also visit classrooms, work on research projects, and interact with graduate

*and undergraduate students, faculty, staff and admin-
istrators . . .* ("Visiting Professors Program" 1988–89, p. 2).

While the following idea can also be applied to women,
institutions might consider hiring minorities who have completed all of their doctoral degree requirements except the
dissertation "and provide a follow-up program of faculty
development that permits the completion of the doctoral
degree" (Green 1989, p. 85). This strategy will ensure the
woman and/or minority doctoral student a guaranteed income
while he or she is completing research for the dissertation,
will assist him or her in gaining some needed experience as
a faculty member, working perhaps under the supervision
of a senior scholar in the department, and will again facilitate
contact by current students with outstanding women and
minorities. Two successful programs are the ABD Seminar Program and the Gaius Charles Bolin Fellowships.

The ABD Seminar Program, developed by the Borough of
Manhattan Community College (and now adopted for sys-
temwide use in the City University of New York's community
colleges), is targeted at full-time minority and women faculty.
The "program has two central features: Faculty can take a
semester's leave at reduced pay to complete their dissertations; weekly seminars—led by senior CUNY faculty—allow
dissertators to give each other criticism and support" ("How
to Turn Your ABDs" 1991, p. 1). In its first year of operation,
five faculty members affiliated with the program completed
their dissertations and received the doctorate.

In 1985, Williams College in Williamstown, Massachusetts,
established the Gaius Charles Bolin Fellowships to "underline
the importance of encouraging able minority students to pursue careers in college teaching [and] enable two minority
graduate students to devote the bulk of their time during the
academic year to the completion of dissertation work"
("Gaius Charles Bolin Fellowships" 1991, p. 11). Terms for
the 1991–92 academic year include $22,000 for housing sup-
port and an allowance of up to $2,000 for research-related
expenses; Bolin Fellows are also "assigned faculty advisers
in the appropriate departments and will be expected to teach
one one-semester course" (p. 11).

Institutional officials should also remember that many
women and minorities initially choose not to enter the field
of higher education after graduation. A recent survey found

that half of all African-Americans who recently earned Ph.D.s did not go into teaching (Cooper and Smith 1990, pp. 10–11). Consequently, institutions should:

Search for senior scholars, who are still active researchers even though they are currently employed outside academe. Hiring retrenchments over the last several years have forced many potential faculty members to seek other careers; some of them (frequently female) have remained productive in their academic fields and would prove competitive candidates. A related strategy is to ensure that research associates and nontenured faculty are seriously considered during searches (studies indicate that many women and minorities have been dead-ended in these positions) (Justus, Freitag, and Parker 1987, p. 40).

Institutional officials also need to look carefully at the cohort of part-time faculty at their institutions when searching for experienced and highly talented women and minority applicants. This group often includes people of color "who would be delighted to apply for full-time positions" (Cooper and Smith 1990, p. 10). In effect, institutions should:

Also invest in programs to recruit women teaching in other segments of education just as they invest in programs to recruit and support athletes. Colleges could identify those with good teaching records who lack the educational background to qualify for university positions. Programs of financial assistance [like] tuition reimbursement, sabbaticals, or other forms of support could be established to assist them in obtaining advanced degrees (Maitland 1990, p. 252).

Unquestionably, some exceptionally innovative and successful long-term and short-term strategies exist for increasing the number of women and minorities in the pipeline. For instance, institutional officials are now strategically targeting marketing and recruitment for future faculty toward a younger audience, including junior high school students who are making initial decisions about careers. In addition, some institutions are developing summer research programs to expose talented women and minority undergraduates to a faculty career through interaction with senior women and minority faculty. As in any high-stakes game, money is an important factor; consequently, guarantees of financial support through undergraduate and graduate school will need to be offered to selected women and minority students; assurances of employment after graduation will probably become a regular component of the financial package that will cause institutional leaders to reconsider the now typically forbidden practice of hiring one's own graduates. In terms of dealing on a short-term basis with the problem of scarce faculty, some institutions are developing faculty exchanges with historically minority and women's institutions and are employing individuals who have completed all doctoral requirements except the dissertation. And institutions need to explore previously untapped markets like business and industry to identify individuals who chose alternative careers but might now be interested in affiliating with a college or university.

Making the Faculty Position an Attractive And Viable Career Option

Unquestionably, women and minorities must view their choice of a faculty position as a viable one in which they will be given every possible opportunity to succeed. In that regard, institutions must make additional support available (for example, networking and opportunities for professional development, which include the availability of a cadre of mentors and sponsors for new women and minority faculty). Every possible strategy should be implemented to provide the assistance needed to help women or minorities achieve tenure and progress steadily through the academic ranks.

"Given the increasing number of nontraditional families in the work force, organizations can no longer expect total dedication, 24-hour commitment, and very high job involvement from all their employees" (Sekaran 1986, p. 69); therefore, institutions must make more overt and sustained attempts to help faculty balance and integrate their work and family lives through providing general support, such as networking and professional development, workshops and counseling related to extraorganizational issues, employment assistance for spouses or partners, salary differentials, and child care.

Networking and opportunities for professional development

A common problem many women and minority faculty report is the feeling of isolation and separation upon affiliation with an institution, particularly, for minority individuals, a predominantly white one. Consequently, institutional officials must work diligently to create opportunities, both on and off campus, where women and minority faculty can interact with their peers both formally and informally. "To counteract their own feelings of isolation, black women faculty need to communicate with black colleagues at other institutions to exchange ideas, discuss research needs, and provide mutual support" (Peterson 1990, p. 34). This same concept applies to all women and to male minority faculty, who should talk with others about constructive solutions to emerging problems to enhance their sense of "belonging" to the institution. Institutions should make efforts to ensure that opportunities for professional growth and development are available for African-American faculty as well as for women and members of other minority groups (Brakeman 1983; Frierson 1990).

Colleges and universities also should provide opportunities for women and minority faculty to meet in preservice or inservice workshops or seminars, with an acknowledged leader, to talk about "values clarification, time and stress management, decision making, gender role socialization, family work sharing, and related topics" (Marshall and Jones 1990, p. 536). Interventions should be aimed at helping women and minorities cope with "family as well as workplace strains. Approaches can involve both programs directed at the individual (i.e., management of family stressors) and those aimed at restructuring the environment to reduce the stress-producing factors (i.e., flexible work hours)" (Baruch, Biener, and Barnett 1987, p. 135). Men and women should work together to identify strategies for coping that will decrease the stress and strain caused by issues of gender that persist in the workplace (Brooker-Gross and Maraffa 1989). Individual and group counseling, provided by the institution, should also be available for women and minority faculty who are experiencing transitions in their careers or their families.

People who are self-reliant, have positive self-concepts, and believe they are in control of their destiny are able to cope with the problems that arise in marriage and parenthood (Pearlin and Schooler 1978); therefore, institutional activities should focus on helping faculty feel more confident in their abilities to deal with internal, workplace, and life-style stressors. "Problems . . . are least likely to result in stress when people remain committed to and involved in those [marriage and parental] relationships" (p. 11).

Perhaps officials in higher education, particularly those at large institutions, should consider establishing centers for minority and women faculty; one model that can be replicated is the Center for Minority Staff Development at Pennsylvania State University. The center provides an opportunity for minority faculty and staff to interact, offers courses dealing with concerns of minorities, provides information on careers to those interested in changing jobs, and helps minorities feel welcome on the campus ("Center Offers Support" 1990).

One large, comprehensive state university in the Northeast has provided formal and informal opportunities for networking for women faculty, positively affecting the environment for women there (Landino and Welch 1990). Informal networking has taken the form of lunches, conversations before and after meetings, sporadic telephone conversations, and quick chats in the hallways. Formal networking has taken place through the Women's Commission.

... institutional activities should focus on helping faculty feel more confident in their abilities to deal with internal, workplace, and life-style stressors.

In the current climate of conservative attitudes about women in higher education, it is difficult for many women in higher education to feel efficacious about their studies and work. [This] networking model supports women by giving them opportunities to see their ideas develop into successful performance accomplishments and the opportunity to see women role models and mentors demonstrate the kind of behavior that results in rewards in the university environment. Moving from the individual perspective to the larger campus community, the networking model provides the women's community with access to information, power, and support so that women are able actually to change their campus environment (Landino and Welch 1990, pp. 18–19).

In addition, minorities and women should be able to develop a variety of relationships with individuals of their own race and gender at the institution through positive and planned mentoring (Anderson and Ramey 1990).

The most intense relationship on the continuum is that of mentor, followed in descending order by sponsors, guides, and, finally, peers. Specifically, mentors are the most pro-

found and paternalistic types of patrons who act as pro-
tectors, benefactors, champions, advocates, and supporters.
Sponsors represent strong patrons who are less powerful
than mentors in promoting and shaping the career of their
proteges; however, both the mentor and sponsor relationships
are hierarchical, parental, strong, and exclusionary. . . .
Further, the guide and peer relationships are more egali-
tarian, are less intense, and allow greater access to a large
number of young professionals. Guides function by explain-
ing the system, pointing out pitfalls and shortcuts, and pro-
viding valuable information concerning the work environ-
ment. . . . Peer relationships can furnish a range of career
functions, such as information sharing, career maneu-
vering, and job-related feedback as well as the psychosocial
functions of confirmation, emotional support, personal
feedback, and friendship (Anglis 1990, pp. 35–37).

The focus of assistance from a designated support person
who could become a mentor:

. . . should be on helping the new faculty member to be suc-
cessful in teaching as well as in his or her scholarly activities.
Providing friendly and immediate help and support in
organizing to teach the courses assigned is often of critical
importance (Arciniega 1990, p. 25).

The exact configuration of the program can vary from a formal
mentoring program, where senior faculty are paired with
junior faculty, to informal "gatherings" of minority and
women faculty so they can discuss common problems and
opportunities; regardless of the vehicle chosen, institutions
must respond to variations in work performance and preferences by providing opportunities for interaction and con-
sultation among the faculty (Lewis and Bierly 1986).

Support for promotion and tenure
Given the multiple demands placed on women and minority
faculty (which can range from excessive involvement in committee work to child care and elder care), schedules for promotion and tenure reviews need to be revised. In effect, "personnel policies should provide a means to stop the tenure
clock for women who bear children [before] receiving tenure" (Hensel 1991, p. 10). Institutional policies should allow

the woman who comes back to work shortly after childbirth to stop the tenure clock for one year and to alternate her work schedule for six months after the child is born (Hensel 1991).

More support for research must also be provided.

We must help new minority [and women] faculty under-stand very well that often rather mystical process so central to our academic ethos—the tenure and promotions process. It is important to make clear not just the written and stated expectations but to assist the newcomer to get started. Help in organizing the [reappointment, promotion, and tenure] file can make a tremendous difference. What should our new colleague know about what is expected with regard to publications and research? How much does effective teaching count? What about service activities? Does the insti-tution really count and take into consideration the con-tributions that such faculty will be making in ethnic- [and gender-]related advising and presentation activities? Which publications count and in which journals? In short, how do things really work around these matters? Related to all this is the need to provide special financial support the first two years for scholarly activities (Arciniega 1990, pp. 25–26).

Clearly, institutions must assist minority and women faculty in dealing with the numerous demands on their time because of their limited numbers; in addition, academic officers must make sure that their contributions are recognized when pro-motion and tenure reviews are conducted. "Clearly, changes need to be made in responsibilities and/or in tenure criteria if the progress of black women faculty is to continue" (Graves 1990, p. 7). Allocating research funds, linking senior profes-sors with junior minority faculty, ensuring that research on minorities is valued, and giving concerted attention to the professional development of the faculty involved are steps in the right direction (Green 1989).

Of utmost importance in ensuring progress toward pro-motion and tenure is early, clear, open, and honest commu-nication about institutional and departmental standards for promotion and tenure. Such discussions indicate that the department and institution are committed to the success of minority or women faculty members and enable junior faculty members to determine priorities and develop plans for satis-fying the various requirements.

Because tenure is such a critical issue in every junior fac-
ulty member's life, it is important that they know exactly
what is expected of them and have a fair opportunity to
meet those expectations. . . . [A number of universities . . .
have approached that problem through orientation sessions
or retreats and handbooks for new faculty. Many depart-
ment chairs also advise new faculty about what is expected
and keep track of their progress] (Justus, Freitag, and Parker
1987, pp. 43–44).

Given women's and minorities' need to have overt support
for research, "department chairs should ensure judicious and
timely use of release time, reduced teaching loads, and assis-
tance/support in preparing fellowship applications" as a
means of ensuring that promotion and tenure will be achieved
(Justus, Freitag, and Parker 1987, p. 12). "[Release time] to
complete a dissertation or an article for publication can be
provided at fairly low cost" (Brakeman 1983, p. 14) and can
help a junior faculty member establish a strong record of
scholarship. The first three years are critical in the success of
minority and women faculty; consequently, administrators
should keep initial responsibilities for teaching and committee service to a minimum (Justus, Freitag, and Parker 1987).
Early sabbatical leaves and extra funding for research for
minorities and women are also important, and institutions
should:

> *. . . provide half-year sabbaticals in the third year. A sab-*
> *batical at this time permits junior faculty members to con-*
> *solidate their work, producing research and publications*
> *in good time for the tenure review process. A new policy*
> *among several Ivy League campuses routinely provides this*
> *sabbatical, and many of their departments manipulate*
> *workloads as well. . . . Use midcareer development awards.*
> *This strategy provides extra funds for research, usually in*
> *the fifth year, particularly in fields [that] have little extra-*
> *mural support . . .* (Justus, Freitag, and Parker 1987, p. 44).

Because of a heavy service load that cuts into research time,
the University of Michigan "has established a development
fund for junior minority faculty for the support of research
proposal development, release time, summer institutes, and
travel" (Frank 1987, pp. 1, 2).

Macalester, Oberlin, and Wabash colleges have implemented special research programs for junior faculty members that include release time for research and support for summer employment (Brakeman 1983). In addition, the Junior Faculty Development Fellowship Program of the Florida Endowment Fund "aims to help blacks and women who work in disciplines in which they are underrepresented" (Green 1989, p. 92). Recipients receive $15,000 to use in supporting activities that "enhance their teaching and their tenure/promotion status at their home institutions" (p. 93).

Providing General Institutional Support

Institutional officials must make concerted and overt efforts to develop support systems that will assist minority or women in deciding to make the faculty their career and in ensuring their success and retention. All institutions must recognize that life-style and family issues affect job satisfaction and productivity; no longer can institutions maintain the stance that what faculty do when they are not at work is of no concern, and they must provide assistance in a variety of forms to help people solve both personal and work-related problems.

Perhaps academic officials need to take a look at some of the corporate benefit programs that now include making telephone lines available for employees' use in contacting their spouses, especially when commuting marriages are involved; further, "it would not be outrageous for academic institutions to help commuting employees in some ways with travel expenses" (Hileman 1990, p. 125). Such vehicles as employment assistance for spouses and partners, the elimination of nepotism laws and differential salaries, and assistance with child care will go far toward ensuring affiliation and retention of the women and minorities who choose to become faculty members in a college or university.

Employment assistance for spouses or partners

The first action an institution concerned with attracting and retaining women and minority faculty should take is to review institutional policies related to nepotism.

Institutions of higher education have in recent years reinterpreted their antinepotism policies . . . to better recruit faculty and administrators, especially those who must relocate. Like the private sector, colleges and universities have been governed by antinepotism rules for years. But given the national competition to identify and recruit faculty and administrators, those rules today are all but gone with the wind. In fact, some institutions have made providing for the "trailing spouse" (the spouse of an individual who is a candidate for a faculty position) a recruitment strategy. The strategy looks especially attractive to colleges and universities interested in diversifying their faculty but faced with a declining pool of minority Ph.D.s. Employing the trailing spouse can offer an effective way of attracting not one but two faculty from underrepresented groups (Morgan 1991, p. 12).

If no positions in the appropriate field are available at the same institution, then academic officials should assist in locating suitable employment for the spouse or partner of the potential faculty member. Not surprisingly, women who rejected offers of faculty positions at various institutions indicated that they were primarily concerned about the job offer and the accommodation of their family's needs (Teevan, Pepper, and Pellizzari 1992). Clearly, as dual-career families become the norm rather than the exception, institutional officials must determine ways to assist couples in finding jobs either in their college or university or at an institution in the geographical area. "Universities definitely trail industry in making such attempts" (Hileman 1990, p. 124); without doubt, the institution that does not consider family issues and spousal employment will surely be the loser in the future. "Virtually everyone . . . [agrees] that the single most important problem in attracting and retaining women and minorities [is] finding jobs for two academics from the same household" (Justus, Freitag, and Parker 1987, p. 42). The Family Employment Program (FEP) developed by Oregon State University is an attempt to help solve many of the problems often encountered by dual-career couples. It has resulted in the employment of many exceptionally talented faculty, including a number of women. "The FEP has three main functions: to facilitate and locate employment opportunities, to coordinate position openings and hiring activities for spouses and partners of new personnel, and to provide resources and referrals for companies desiring assistance with spousal employment" (Stafford and Spanier 1990, p. 39). In addition to assistance with employment, the institution also provides several perks for spouses and partners.

Spouses are eligible for library services equivalent to those of faculty members, staff parking privileges, and the services of the Career Planning and Placement Office, including access to reference materials and advice on resume preparation and employment interviewing. In addition, a faculty fellowship is made available to qualified academic spouses (i.e., generally those with terminal degrees in their fields). These fellowships, which carry a minimum one-time stipend of $12,000 plus fringe benefits, provide a part-time salaried appointment for one year only (or nine months where appropriate) (Stafford and Spanier 1990, p. 41).

Institutions should improve "job referrals outside faculty positions" to interested spouses and partners (Brooker-Gross and Maraffa 1989, p. 42). Services such as the ones provided through the FEP at Oregon State University provide evidence that the full resources of the institution are available to assist women or minorities and their spouses in adjusting to the academic climate and in making the transition as easy as possible for everyone involved.

Salary differentials
The institution must also decide its stance on above-market salaries for women and minorities (Green 1989). In other words, the institution must decide whether it is willing to pay a minority or woman faculty member more than a majority candidate or even an existing majority faculty member with equivalent or more experience. To recruit a candidate actively and then fall short when it comes to negotiating salary is problematic, and administrators should decide salary issues at the outset.

Child care
Locating top-quality, flexible child-care arrangements is a major problem for women and minority faculty who must juggle the responsibilities of being a professional, a parent, and a spouse. Institutional officials should thus make every effort to eliminate this issue from the prospective faculty member's consideration. College and university officials either

must provide assistance in locating child care (possibly sub-sidizing it) or provide quality, on-site child care for employees and students (Scarr, Phillips, and McCartney 1989).

> *Most academic women of my generation gave up the priv-ilege of child bearing in the interests of their careers. Most graduate student women today state that they are unwilling to pay such a price; however, universities have been unhelp-ful to husband/wife or wife/husband couples and have done little in the area of child care* (Stern 1990, p. 52).

Providing Incentives to Diversify the Faculty
All of the strategies discussed in this section assume a com-mitment by individuals in the institution to the development and retention of a diverse faculty. All administrative officials must clearly demonstrate this commitment, which should include "incentives to hire minority faculty through extra fac-ulty slots or additional departmental monies" (Green 1989, p. 86). "Awards of positions (FTEs) should be considered for departments who identify outstanding minority or women faculty even when they do not fit a specialty. This strategy has proven the most effective incentive for affirmative action hir-ing" (Justus, Freitag, and Parker 1987, p. 14) at institutions like the University of California, the State University of New York, Miami University of Ohio, the University of Wisconsin–Madison, and Bowling Green State University in Ohio.

The University of California developed its Targets of Oppor-tunity Program (TOP) as one means of increasing the number of minorities and women on the faculty. Specifically, the pro-gram "allocates an additional position to a department to recruit a minority or woman candidate who, while meeting accepted academic standards, does not match an established position description. This strategy enables a department to seize an opportunity to diversify its faculty that might other-wise be lost" (Justus, Freitag, and Parker 1987, pp. 38–39).

Similarly, the SUNY system implemented its Underrepre-sented Faculty Initiative, which allows departments to seize the opportunity to employ minority faculty when they are available instead of only when an opening exists. Once hired, the individual's salary is paid by the system and institution on a sliding scale over three years; at the end of three years, "the institution must provide a vacant tenure-track slot—either through an internal transfer, death, contract nonrenewal, or retirement—and the resources for that slot" ("Recruiting Minority Faculty" 1990, p. 1).

Another plan that institutions can model is the Voluntary Affirmative Action Plan for Black and Other Minority Faculty that has been in place at Miami University of Ohio since 1983. The plan allows for direct recruitment and hiring of minority candidates in instances of historical exclusion or past discrimination and uses additional tenure-track lines as incentives for departments to identify African-Americans and other members of minority groups for open positions.* The plan is modeled after the U.S. Supreme Court's 1979 *Weber* decision, in which an employer must identify a conspicuous racial imbalance in his or her work force and develop a specific plan of action to correct such racial imbalance; further, the plan must be temporary, lasting only as long as necessary to eliminate manifest racial imbalance. Under the Voluntary Affirmative Action Plan, a department that previously did not have a minority faculty member may fill a vacant position without a full search by identifying a qualified African-American or other minority candidate as long as the candidate is accepted by a majority vote of the departmental faculty. Individual departments that decide to participate are eligible only if the availability of African-American or other minorities equals one or more positions within the department and if they have never hired a tenure-track faculty member from the minority group. A department becomes ineligible as soon as the representation of African-Americans and other minority faculty within the department is equal to their respective availability. Miami University also established a diversification fund in 1981 to help bring women and minority candidates to the campus for interviews and to provide salary supplements.**

Recruitment at Miami University has been successful; since 1981, the university has raised the number of African-American professors from seven to 33 and the number of African-American administrators and professional staff from 12 to 36. Since 1981, women have averaged over 40 percent of all new tenurable faculty hires, and the number of women academic department chairs and administrators has increased from two to 12.

---

*Gary Hunter, director of affirmative action, 30 November 1990, personal communication.
**Gary Hunter 4 August 1992, personal communication.

The University of Wisconsin–Madison took various steps to implement a plan to increase minority faculty and staff. In terms of faculty, the goal established in 1988 was to hire 70 minority female and male faculty by September 1991, which necessitated more than doubling the number of existing minority faculty. The university used some of the following strategies to create greater diversity on campus.

1. Minorities, whenever possible, replace faculty who retire or resign. The institutional goal is to add 15 tenure-track junior faculty each year (for a total of 45 of the 70).
2. For new positions (authorized in the 1988–89 state budget), efforts are made to work with deans and department heads to ensure that the recruitment of minority and women candidates receives top priority. Departments that have outstanding candidates are assured of the opportunity to recruit them. Further, research support from the graduate school is available for recruited faculty. The institution's goal was to add 25 outstanding senior, tenured, minority faculty by September 1991.
3. Available positions are used (before hiring is completed) to draw male and female minority faculty from other institutions as semester or academic-year visitors while retaining long-term hiring goals. The goal was to attract at least 15 such visitors for the 1988–89 academic year ("The Madison Plan" 1988).

As of fall 1991, the university had hired 62 new targeted minority faculty, of whom 21 were African-American, six were American Indian, and 35 were Hispanic. Seven African-American, nine Hispanic, and three American Indian faculty were lost to other institutions, retirement, and nonretention. Thus, the net increase in minority faculty was 43. In addition to the 62 targeted faculty who were hired, the university has also employed 38 Asian-American faculty since the inception of the plan.*

By providing restricted funds for hiring minorities, Bowling Green State University increased the number of minority faculty affiliated with the institution. Specifically, the institution:

---

*A. Ally 6 August 1992, personal communication.

*. . . set aside $300,000 to assist departments and programs
in attracting minority faculty to the campus. . . . With
money from the program, college deans and department
chairs have the additional resources to attract the very best
minority faculty. For [1990–91], nine African-Americans,
two Hispanics, and three Asian/Pacific Islanders joined the
staff. In all, 22 African-Americans, five Hispanics, and 42
Asian/Pacific Islanders [were] teaching at the university
[in 1990–91]* ("Minority Faculty Recruiting" 1990, p. 6).

The University of Michigan's Target of Opportunity Fund
has also been highly successful in the institution's efforts to
recruit and retain minority faculty.

*Established in the spring of 1987, the fund makes money
available from the General Fund to departments and units
with an opportunity to appoint an underrepresented senior-
level faculty member, regardless of whether a position is
open that matches the faculty member's academic interest*
(Seidman 1990a, p. 4).

In addition to the designation of supplemental positions
for minorities and women, other strategies have been used
to support institutional attempts to diversify faculty, such as
providing supplemental monies to ensure the competitiveness
of salaries and ensuring that recruitment captures the attention
of people from a variety of multicultural and multiethnic backgrounds. The programs in place at Wayne State University and
Long Beach City College can be replicated on other campuses.
Wayne State University sets aside $150,000 annually "to
assure that incentives would be available to attract talented
minority faculty and administrators. Any unused portion of
the annual allocation is used to supplement the Minority Faculty Research Awards" (Minority Resource Center 1990, p. 33).
Known as the Provost's Minority Faculty Recruitment Fund,
the monies ensure that competitive offers can be made to
selected minority candidates.
Of the newly hired faculty at Long Beach City College during academic year 1989–90, nearly half were minorities. Using
funds made available by the state, LBCC implemented several
new strategies, including the development and distribution
of a publication aimed at minority administrators and faculty,

the advertising of positions in publications serving a diverse audience, and the garnering of support from leaders of three local minority organizations ("Recruiting Minority Faculty" 1990, p. 2). Administrators believe that the involvement of minority leaders in recruitment was the most important communication strategy used; specifically, they said, "the leaders made us more believable in the community" (p. 2).

Clearly, success abounds when institutions make it worth the effort for faculty and department heads to engage in the process of recruiting women and minority candidates now in the academic pipeline. Consequently, leaders in all post-secondary institutions need to determine ways to stimulate creative thinking and, without a doubt, must earmark funds to ensure the availability of positions for minorities and women whenever the opportunity arises to employ them.

Summary

"Unless there is a radical change in how we do business, we cannot hope to improve materially the representation of minorities on our faculties . . . " (Stern 1990, p. 52). In this competitive market for women and minorities, such a radical change can be achieved only through the creative deployment of resources in conjunction with innovative ways of attracting and retaining talented women and minority faculty. Clearly, some institutions have been successful in increasing the number of women and minorities on their faculties, and others in the academy should carefully consider the strategies they use. While some minimal success has been achieved, however, room for innovation and commitment certainly still exists.

To ensure that today's students have an opportunity to interact with minority and women faculty, institutions can develop faculty exchanges or visiting lecturer programs with historically minority or women's colleges. They also can consider hiring individuals who are nearing completion of a doctoral degree but have not finished their dissertation; in addition, they can contact individuals now employed in alternative markets to determine whether a faculty position is now a viable career for them. While implementing these short-term strategies, institutional officials will also have to deal aggressively with the problem of the pipeline: (1) by marketing a career in the faculty to young men and women as they make initial choices about a career; (2) by designing opportunities for talented high school and undergraduate women and minorities to work with faculty to conduct research; and (3) by providing full-tuition undergraduate and graduate scholarships, fellowships, and/or assistantships as well as guarantees of employment after completion of the doctorate to women and minorities who agree to enter the faculty.

Institutional officials and faculty must also be sure that a faculty career is attractive to women and minorities and that the environment where they work will be conducive to job satisfaction and ultimate success. Consequently, networks and opportunities for professional development must abound. An intricate system of sabbaticals, release time for research, reduced teaching and committee loads, and flexible promotion and tenure schedules should be in place to ensure that minority or women faculty members can in fact achieve tenure and full professorial rank, and the institution must be dedicated to developing an environment in which women and minority faculty are satisfied with the various facets of their work. For example, the institution might need to pay above-market salaries to attract targeted women and minorities to the faculty; consequently, it must develop policies regarding salary differentials. Moreover, the institution must offer a support structure that includes appealing personal benefits as well. The college or university, for example, can assist the spouse or partner of the faculty member involved to locate suitable employment. The institution should also consider either providing child care or establishing referral systems to help minority and women faculty who need such services.

In the future, institutional officials will be required to pay more than lip service to hiring, developing, and retaining women and minority faculty. Unquestionably, the overt and consistent commitment of the chief executive will help to ensure the success of recruitment and retention (Justus, Freitag, and Parker 1987). "Although colleges and universities will vary in their approach to recruitment and retention of faculty of color, any successful effort must start with the institution's president . . . " (Conciatore 1991, p. 46). No one person can cause the massive change needed in higher education, however. While today's faculty must shoulder the major responsibility for diversifying the faculty of the future (Justus, Freitag, and Parker 1987), administrators and trustees must provide

"Although colleges and universities will vary in their approach to recruitment and retention of faculty of color, any successful effort must start with the institution's president. . . ."

the resources and leadership needed to succeed. Furthermore, women and minorities in top administrative and academic positions must push to see that equity is achieved.

> *Only a few blacks are in top-level administrative and academic positions in predominantly white institutions. Some of these persons may possess a great deal of power, influence, and authority. It seems incumbent upon them to utilize their leverage by virtue of the authority of the position occupied to influence decisions in ways that will result in greater equity with respect to recruitment, hiring, promotion, retention, and salary distribution. They should monitor institutional records in these areas. They should note any evidence of race-based inequities and use their authority and influence to prevent unfair practices and, simultaneously, facilitate equity in recruitment, hiring, promotion, and salary policies . . .* (Blackwell 1983, pp. 69–70).

Unquestionably, everyone involved in postsecondary education must recognize the significant need for and the benefits of employing women and minorities in the faculty. "The key to an institution's success is making hiring for diversity a real institutional priority" (Cooper and Smith 1990, p. 10). Once an institution makes a commitment, all parties must work together to enhance job satisfaction by ensuring equal opportunity in hiring, promotion, tenure, salary, and retention. And institutional officials must provide the necessary support to create satisfaction with various aspects of the faculty position and must help women and minority faculty cope with the almost overwhelming demands of having a family and a full-time faculty career.

REFERENCES

The Educational Resources Information Center (ERIC) Clearinghouse on Higher Education abstracts and indexes the current literature on higher education for inclusion in ERIC's data base and announcement in ERIC's monthly bibliographic journal, *Resources in Education* (RIE). Most of these publications are available through the ERIC Document Reproduction Service (EDRS). For publications cited in this bibliography that are available from EDRS, ordering number and price code are included. Readers who wish to order a publication should write to the ERIC Document Reproduction Service, 7420 Fullerton Rd., Suite 110, Springfield, VA 22153-2852. (Phone orders with VISA or MasterCard are taken at 800-443-ERIC or 703-440-1400.) When ordering, please specify the document (ED) number. Documents are available as noted in microfiche (MF) and paper copy (PC). If you have the price code ready when you call EDRS, an exact price can be quoted. The last page of the latest issue of *Resources in Education* also has the current cost, listed by code.

Aisenberg, N., and M. Harrington. 1988. *Women of Academe: Outsiders in the Sacred Grove.* Amherst: Univ. of Massachusetts Press.

Alderfer, C. 1967. "An Organizational Syndrome." *Administrative Science Quarterly* 12: 440–60.

Amatea, E.S., and E.G. Cross. 1981. "Competing Worlds, Competing Standards: Personal Control for the Professional Career Woman, Wife, and Mother." *Journal of the National Association of Women Deans, Administrators, and Counselors* 44: 3–10.

American Association of State Colleges and Universities. 1990. *Faculty at Public Four-Year Institutions: A Continuing Profile.* Special Report. Washington, D.C.: Author.

American Association of University Professors. March/April 1992. "Diversity within Adversity: The Annual Report on the Economic Status of the Profession, 1991–92." *Academe* 77: 7–52.

Andersen, C.J., D.J. Carter, and A.G. Malizio. 1989. *1989–90 Fact Book on Higher Education.* New York: ACE/Macmillan.

Anderson, R. 1984. "Role Perceptions and Occupational Self-Esteem of Female University Administrators." Ph.D. dissertation, Bowling Green State Univ.

Anderson, R., and P. Ramey. 1990. "Women in Higher Education: Development through Administrative Mentoring." In *Women in Higher Education: Changes and Challenges,* edited by Lynne B. Welch. New York: Praeger.

Andrulis, D., M. Sikes, and T. Friedman. Winter 1975. "Black Professionals in Predominantly White Institutions of Higher Education: An Examination of Some Demographic and Mobility Characteristics." *Journal of Negro Education* 44: 6–11.

Anglis, C. 1990. "Career Advancement Strategies of Selected Female Vice Presidents and Presidents of Higher Education Institutions in a Midwestern State." Ph.D. dissertation, Bowling

Green State Univ.

Archbold, P.G. 1983. "Impact of Parent-Caring on Women." *Family Relations* 32: 39–46.

Arciniega, T. 1990. "The Challenge of Developing Effective Strategies to Recruit and Retain Ethnic Minority Faculty." Paper presented at California Community Colleges Faculty and Staff Conference, San Diego, California. ED 320 516. 30 pp. MF–01; PC–02.

Astin, A. 1982. *Minorities in American Higher Education.* San Francisco: Jossey-Bass.

Astin, H.S., and A.E. Bayer. 1973. "Sex Discrimination in Academe." In *Academic Women on the Move,* edited by A.S. Rossi and A. Calderwood. New York: Russell Sage Foundation.

Astin, H.S., and M. Snyder. July/August 1982. "Affirmative Action 1972–1982: A Decade of Response." *Change* 14: 28–31+.

Austin, A., and Z. Gamson. 1983. *Academic Workplace: New Demands, Heightened Tensions.* ASHE-ERIC Higher Education Report No. 10. Washington, D.C.: Association for the Study of Higher Education. ED 243 397. 131 pp. MF–01; PC–06.

Austin, A.E., and M. Pilat. January/February 1990. "Tension, Stress, and the Tapestry of Faculty Lives." *Academe* 1: 38–42.

Baruch, G.K., L. Biener, and R.C. Barnett. 1987. "Women and Gender in Research on Work and Family Stress." *American Psychologist* 42: 131–36.

Bass, B., and G. Barrett. 1975. *Man, Work, and Organizations.* Boston: Allyn & Bacon.

Ben-Porat, A. 1981. "Event and Agent: Toward a Structural Theory of Job Satisfaction." *Personnel Psychology* 34: 523–34.

Benton, S.Y. 1986. "Women Administrators in the 1980s: A New Breed." In *Strategies and Attitudes: Women in Educational Administration,* edited by P.A. Farrant. Washington, D.C.: National Association of Women Deans, Administrators, and Counselors. ED 285 439. 197 pp. MF–01; PC not available EDRS.

Bess, J. 1981. "Intrinsic Satisfaction from Academic versus Other Professional Work: A Comparative Analysis." Paper read at an annual meeting of the Association for the Study of Higher Education, Washington, D.C. ED 203 805. 52 pp. MF–01; PC–03.

Biernat, M., and C.B. Wortman. 1991. "Sharing of Home Responsibilities between Professionally Employed Women and Their Husbands." *Journal of Personality and Social Psychology* 60: 844–60.

Billingsley, A. 1982. "Building Strong Faculties in Black Colleges." *Journal of Negro Education* 51: 4–15.

Birnbaum, R. 1984. "The Effects of a Neutral Third Party on Academic Bargaining Relationships and Campus Climate." *Journal of Higher Education* 55: 719–34.

Black, A. Summer 1981. "Affirmative Action and the Black Academic Situation." *Western Journal of Black Studies* 5: 87–94.

Black Issues in Higher Education 7 (January 1991): 11, 51–52.

Black Issues in Higher Education 8 (January 1992): 28, 35.

Blackwell, J. 1983. "Strategies for Improving the Status of Blacks in Higher Education." *Planning and Changing* 14: 56–73.

Boberg, A., and R. Blackburn. 1983. "Faculty Work Dissatisfactions and Their Concern for Quality." Paper read at an annual forum of the Association for Institutional Research, Toronto, Ontario. ED 232 570. 26 pp. MF–01; PC–02.

Bornheimer, D. 1985. "Conditions Influencing Faculty Voting in Collective Bargaining Elections." *Research in Higher Education* 22: 291–305.

Bowen, H., and J. Schuster. 1986. *American Professors: A National Resource Imperiled.* New York: Oxford Univ. Press.

Bowles, F., and F. Decosta. 1971. *Between Two Worlds: A Profile of Negro Higher Education.* New York: McGraw-Hill.

Boyd, W.M. January/February 1989. "Affirmative Action: A Way to Win." *AGB Reports* 31: 22–25.

Brakeman, L. March 1983. "Hiring and Keeping the Best Faculty." In *New Directions for Higher Education* No. 41, edited by Jon W. Fuller. San Francisco: Jossey-Bass.

Brody, E.M., M.H. Kleban, P.T. Johnsen, C. Hoffman, and C.B. Schoonover. 1987. "Work Status and Parent Care: A Comparison of Four Groups of Women." *Gerontologist* 27: 201–8.

Brooker-Gross, S.R., and T.A. Maraffa. 1989. "Faculty Spouses: Their Post-Migration Job Searches." *Initiatives* 52: 37–43.

Brown, D. 1967. *The Mobile Professors.* Washington, D.C.: American Council on Education.

Brown, S. 1988. *Increasing Minority Faculty: An Elusive Goal.* Princeton, N.J.: Educational Testing Service. ED 299 904. 38 pp. MF–01; PC–02.

Bureau of Institutional Research. 1974. "University of Illinois Employees Job Satisfaction Study." Champaign: Univ. of Illinois, Educational Resources Information Center. ED 132 902. 74 pp. MF–01; PC–03.

Burke, R.J. 1987. "Part VI. Conclusion: The Present and Future Status of Stress Research." In *Job Stress: From Theory to Suggestion,* edited by J. Ivancevich and D.C. Ganster. New York: Haworth Press.

Burrell, L. 1980. "Is There a Future for Black Students on Predominantly White Campuses?" *Integrated Education* 18: 23–27.

Campbell, J., and R. Pritchard. 1976. "Motivation Theory in Industrial and Organizational Psychology." In *Handbook of Industrial and Organizational Psychology,* edited by M. Dunnette. Chicago: Rand McNally.

Caplan, R. 1987a. "Person-Environment Fit in Organizations: Theories, Facts, and Values." In *Occupational Stress and Organizational Effectiveness,* edited by A. Riley and S. Zaccaro. New York: Praeger.

———. 1987b. "Person-Environment Fit Theory and Organizations:

Commensurate Dimensions, Time Perspective, and Mechanisms."
Journal of Vocational Behavior 31: 248–67.

Carnegie Commission on Higher Education. 1973. *Opportunities for Women in Higher Education.* New York: McGraw-Hill.

Carnegie Foundation for the Advancement of Teaching. 1986. "The Satisfied Faculty." *Change* 18: 31–34.

———. 1989. *The Condition of the Professoriate: Attitudes and Trends, 1989.* Princeton, N.J.: Princeton Univ. Press. ED 312 963. 162 pp. MF–01; PC not available EDRS.

Cavenar, M. 1987. "Factors Influencing Job Satisfaction and Retention among Faculty Members in Schools of Nursing Offering the Ph.D. Degree." Ph.D. dissertation, Univ. of North Carolina.

"Center Offers Support to Minority Staff." 10 December 1990. *Administrator* 9: 1–2.

Chung, K. 1977. *Motivational Theories and Practices.* Columbus, Ohio: Grid, Inc.

Clark, B. June/July 1989. "The Absorbing Errand." *Educational Researcher* 18: 1–14.

Clark, S.M., M. Corcoran, and D.R. Lewis. 1986. "The Case for an Institutional Perspective on Faculty Development." *Journal of Higher Education* 57: 176–95.

Cohen, A. 1973. "Work Satisfaction among Junior College Faculty Members." Paper read at an annual meeting of the California Educational Research Association, Los Angeles, California. ED 081 426. 8 pp. MF–01; PC–01.

———. 1974. "Community College Faculty Job Satisfaction." *Research in Higher Education* 2: 369–76.

Conciatore, J. January 1991. "Faculty Recruitment and Retention Starts with CEOs, Educators Say." *Black Issues in Higher Education* 7: 46–47.

Cooper, R., and B. Smith. October 1990. "Achieving a Diverse Faculty." *AAHE Bulletin* 43: 10–12.

Cox, J. 1982. "Comparisons of Leadership Styles and Personal Characteristics of Middle- and Upper-Level Women Administrators in Higher Education and Corporate Business." Ph.D. dissertation, Georgia State Univ.

Crawford, M. 1982. "In Pursuit of the Well-Rounded Life: Women Scholars and the Family." In *Handbook for Women Scholars: Strategies for Success,* edited by M.L. Spencer, M. Kehoe, and K. Speece. San Francisco: Center for Women Scholars.

Crawford, S. 1987. "Perceptions about Workplace Factors That Affect Professional Growth of Female Faculty in Traditional and Nontraditional Disciplines." Ph.D. dissertation, Bowling Green State Univ.

Curry-Williams, M. 1985. "Factors That Influence 'Other-Race' Faculty Decisions to Accept, Remain In, and Consider Leaving Faculty Positions at Four Southeastern Public Universities." Ph.D. dissertation,

Virginia Polytechnic Institute and State Univ.

Davis, L. 1985. "Black and White Social Work Faculty: Perceptions of Respect, Satisfaction, Job Permanence." *Journal of Sociology and Social Welfare* 12: 79–94.

Dean, D.L. 1986. "Comparison of Self-Perceived Leadership Styles of Women in Higher Education and Noneducation Management Positions." Ph.D. dissertation, Oregon State Univ.

Dennis, L. Fall 1982. "Why Not Merit Pay?" *Contemporary Education* 54: 18–21.

Diener, T. 1984. "College Faculty and Job Satisfaction." Paper presented at an annual meeting of the American Educational Research Association, New Orleans, Louisiana. ED 248 820. 23 pp. MF–01; PC–01.

Douglas, J. 1991. *Directory of Faculty Contracts and Bargaining Agents in Institutions of Higher Education.* New York: CUNY, Baruch College, National Center for the Study of Collective Bargaining in Higher Education and the Professions. ED 335 981. 284 pp. MF–01; PC not available EDRS.

Eckert, R., and J. Stecklein. 1961. *Job Motivations and Satisfactions of College Teachers: A Study of Faculty Members in Minnesota Colleges.* Washington, D.C.: U.S. Government Printing Office.

Edmundson, J. 1969. *An Identification of Selected Items Associated with Faculty Job Satisfaction in the North Carolina System of Community Colleges.* Raleigh: North Carolina State Univ. ED 045 940. 90 pp. MF–01; PC–04.

Elmore, C., and R. Blackburn. 1983. "Black and White Faculty in White Research Universities." *Journal of Higher Education* 54: 1–15.

Epps, E. September/October 1989. "Academic Culture and the Minority Professor." *Academe* 75: 23–26.

Etaugh, C. 1984. "Women Faculty and Administrators in Higher Education: Changes in Their Status since 1972." *Journal of the National Association of Women Deans, Administrators, and Counselors* 48: 21–25.

Ethington, C.A., J.C. Smart, and M.L. Zeltmann. 1989. "Institutional Satisfaction of Women Faculty." *Research in Higher Education* 30: 261–71.

Farley, J. 1982. *Academic Women and Employment Discrimination.* Ithaca, N.Y.: Cornell Univ. ED 220 550. 108 pp. MF–01; PC not available EDRS.

Fassiotto, M. 1986. "The Merit of Merit: Notes on the Arguments for and against Merit Systems." Draft of a paper presented to the Faculty Senate of Chaminade Univ., Honolulu, Hawaii. ED 271 040. 25 pp. MF–01; PC–01.

Feuille, P., and J. Blandin. 1974. "Faculty Job Satisfaction and Bargaining Sentiments: A Case Study." *Academy of Management Journal* 17: 678–92.

Finkelstein, M. 1978. "Three Decades of Research on American Academics: A Descriptive Portrait and Synthesis of Findings." Ph.D. dissertation, State Univ. of New York–Buffalo.

————. 1987. "Women and Minority Faculty." In *ASHE Reader on Faculty and Faculty Issues in Colleges and Universities,* edited by M. Finkelstein. 2d rev. ed. Lexington, Mass.: Ginn Press.

Fleming, J. 1984. *Blacks in College.* San Francisco: Jossey-Bass.

"Florida Endowment Fund for Higher Education in Florida Announces." 22 November 1990. *Black Issues in Higher Education* 7: 12.

Fox, M.F. 1984. "Women and Higher Education: Sex Differentials in the Status of Students and Scholars." In *Women: A Feminist Perspective,* edited by J. Freeman. Mountain View, Calif.: Mayfield Publishing Co.

Fox, M.F., and S. Hesse-Biber. 1984. *Women at Work.* Mountain View, Calif.: Mayfield Publishing Co.

Frank, M. 19 November 1987. "Moody, the Recruiter, Enlisting All Universities in Diversity Efforts." *University Record* 43: 1.

Freeman, B. 1977. "Faculty Women in the American University: Up the Down Staircase." *Higher Education* 6: 165–88.

Freeman, G.E. 1977. "A Profile of Top-Level Women Administrators in Higher Education in Washington, D.C." Study conducted as requirement for Ed.D. degree. ED 144 472. 33 pp. MF–01; PC–02.

French, J., Jr., C. Tupper, and E. Mueller. 1965. "Workload of University Professors." Mimeographed. Ann Arbor: Univ. of Michigan. ED 003 329. 278 pp. MF–01; PC–12.

Frierson, H., Jr. 1990. "The Situation of Black Educational Researchers: Continuation of a Crisis." *Educational Researcher* 19: 12–17.

Fuchs, R., and J. Lovano-Kerr. 1981. "Retention, Professional Development, and Quality of Life: A Comparative Study of Male/Female Nontenured Faculty." Paper presented at an annual meeting of the American Educational Research Association, Los Angeles, California. ED 202 416. 26 pp. MF–01; PC–02.

Fulton, B.F. 1986. "Access for Minorities and Women to Administrative Leadership Positions: Influence of the Search Committee." In *Strategies and Attitudes: Women in Educational Administration,* edited by P.A. Farrant. Washington, D.C.: National Association of Women Deans, Administrators, and Counselors.

"Gaius Charles Bolin Fellowships for Minority Graduate Students." 17 January 1991. *Black Issues in Higher Education* 7: 11.

Gappa, J.M., and B.S. Uehling. 1979. *Women in Academe: Steps to Greater Equality.* AAHE-ERIC Higher Education Research Report No. 1. Washington, D.C.: American Association for Higher Education. ED 169 873. 97 pp. MF–01; PC–04.

Garza, H. Winter 1988. "The 'Barrioization' of Hispanic Faculty." *Educational Record* 69: 122–24.

Glowinkowski, S.P., and C.L. Cooper. 1987. "Managers and Professionals in Business/Industrial Settings: The Research Evidence." In *Job Stress: From Theory to Suggestion,* edited by J. Ivancevich and D.C. Ganster. Binghamton, N.Y.: Haworth Press.

Gmelch, W.H. July 1988. "Research Perspectives on Administrative Stress: Causes, Reactions, Responses, and Consequences." *Journal of Educational Administration* 26: 477–90.

Gmelch, W.H., N.P. Lovrich, and P.K. Wilke. 1984. "Sources of Stress in Academe: A National Perspective." *Research in Higher Education* 20: 477–90. ED 232 518. 28 pp. MF–01; PC–02.

Gmelch, W.H., P.K. Wilke, and N.P. Lovrich. 1986. "Dimensions of Stress among University Faculty: Factor-Analytic Results from a National Study." *Research in Higher Education* 24: 266–86.

Graham, P.A. 1971. "Women in Academe." In *The Professional Woman,* edited by A. Theodore. Cambridge, Mass.: Schenkman Publishing.

———. 1973. "Status Transitions of Women Students, Faculty, and Administrators." In *Academic Women on the Move,* edited by A.S. Rossi and A. Calderwood. New York: Russell Sage Foundation.

Grahn, J., et al. 1981. "General College Job Satisfaction Survey, University of Minnesota. Summer 1980." Minneapolis: Univ. of Minnesota, General College. ED 208 716. 28 pp. MF–01; PC–02.

Graves, S.B. 1990. "A Case of Double Jeopardy? Black Women in Higher Education." *Initiatives* 53 (Special Issue: Black Women in Higher Education): 3–8.

Green, M., ed. 1989. *Minorities on Campus: A Handbook for Enhancing Diversity.* Washington, D.C.: American Council on Education.

Gustad, J. 1960. *The Career Decisions of College Teachers.* SREB Research Monograph Series No. 2. Atlanta: Southern Regional Education Board.

Hackman, J.R., and G.R. Oldham. 1980. *Work Design.* Reading, Mass.: Addison-Wesley.

Halcomb, R. 1979. *Women Making It: Patterns and Profiles of Success.* New York: Atheneum.

Hall, M., and W. Allen. 1983. "Race Consciousness and Achievement: Two Issues in the Study of Black Graduate/Professional Students." *Integrated Education* 20: 56–61.

Halpin, A. 1959. *The Leadership Behavior of School Superintendents.* Chicago: Univ. of Chicago, Midwest Administration Center.

Hammond, L. 1988. "Mediators of Stress and Role Satisfaction in Multiple-Role Women." Paper read at an annual meeting of the Western Psychological Association, April 28–May 1, Burlingame, California. ED 298 376. 26 pp. MF–01; PC–02.

Harrison, M. 1979. "Job Satisfaction among Faculty Members in a Large Black Southern University." Ph.D. dissertation, Louisiana State Univ. and Agricultural and Mechanical College.

Harvey, W., and D. Scott-Jones. Summer 1985. "We Can't Find Any:

The Elusiveness of Black Faculty Members in American Higher
Education." *Issues in Education* 3: 68–76.

Hellriegel, D., and J. Slocum, Jr. June 1974. "Organizational Climate:
Measures, Research, and Contingencies." *Academy of Management
Journal* 17: 255–80.

Hensel, N. 1990. "Maternity, Promotion, and Tenure: Are They Com-
patible?" In *Women in Higher Education: Changes and Challenges,*
edited by L.B. Welch. New York: Praeger.

———. 1991. *Realizing Gender Equality in Higher Education: The
Need to Integrate Work/Family Issues.* ASHE-ERIC Higher Education
Report No. 2. Washington, D.C.: George Washington Univ., School
of Education and Human Development. ED 338 128. 122 pp. MF–
01; PC–05.

Hersey, P., and K. Blanchard. 1988. *Management of Organizational
Behavior: Utilizing Human Resources.* Englewood Cliffs, N.J.:
Prentice-Hall.

Herzberg, F. 1966. *Work and the Nature of Man.* New York: World
Publishing Co.

———. 1972. *Work and the Nature of Man.* Reprint. New York:
World Publishing Co.

Herzberg, F., B. Mausner, R. Peterson, and D. Capwell. 1957. *Job Attitudes: A Review of Research and Opinion.* Pittsburgh: Psychological
Service of Pittsburgh.

Herzberg, F., B. Mausner, and B. Snyderman. 1959. *The Motivation
to Work.* 2d rev. ed. New York: John Wiley & Sons.

Hickman, J. 1986. "A Comparison of the Relationship of Faculty Perceptions of Organizational Climate to Expressed Job Satisfaction
in Baccalaureate Degree Nursing Programs." Ph.D. dissertation,
Temple Univ.

Hileman, S. 1990. "The 'Female-Determined Relationship': Personal
and Professional Needs of Academic Women in Commuter Marriages." In *Women in Higher Education,* edited by L.B. Welch. New
York: Praeger.

Hill, M.D. 1982. "Variations in Job Satisfaction among Higher Education Faculty in Unionized and Nonunionized Institutions in
Pennsylvania." *Journal of Collective Negotiations* 11: 165–80.

———. 1983. "Some Factors Affecting the Job Satisfaction of Academic Women." Paper read at an annual meeting of the American
Educational Research Association, Montreal, Quebec. ED 231 297.
28 pp. MF–01; PC–02.

———. 1984a. "Faculty Sex Composition and Job Satisfaction among
Academic Women." Paper read at an annual meeting of the American Educational Research Association, New York, New York. ED
215 632. 29 pp. MF–01; PC not available EDRS.

———. March/April 1984b. "Faculty Sex Composition and Job
Satisfaction of Academic Women." *International Journal of
Women's Studies* 1: 179–89. ED 215 632. 10 pp. MF–01; PC not

available EDRS.

———. 1987. "A Theoretical Analysis of Faculty Job Satisfaction/Dis-
satisfaction." *Educational Research Quarterly:* 10: 36–44.

Hilton, D. 1985. "Identification of Satisfying and Dissatisfying Factors
and Determination of Level of Job Satisfaction for Postsecondary
Vocational Education Faculty in Public Supported Institutions in
Idaho." Ph.D. dissertation, Univ. of Idaho.

Hollon, C., and G. Gemmill. Winter 1976. "A Comparison of Female
and Male Professors on Participation in Decision Making, Job-
Related Tension, Job Involvement, and Job Satisfaction." *Educational Administration Quarterly* 12: 80–93.

"How to Turn Your ABDs into Ph.D.s." January 1991. *Academic Leader*
7: 1.

Hulin, C.L., and P.C. Smith. 1964. "Sex Differences in Job Satisfaction."
Journal of Applied Psychology 48: 88–92.

Hunter, M., J. Ventimiglia, and M. Crow. March/April 1980. "Faculty
Morale in Higher Education." *Journal of Teacher Education* 31:
27–30.

Ibrahim, J. 1985. "Job Satisfaction of Faculty Members at Selected
Southern Universities." Ph.D. dissertation, Univ. of Southern
Mississippi.

Institute for Research in Social Behavior. 1978. "University of California Faculty Time-Use Study: Report for the 1977–1978 Academic
Year." Berkeley: Author. ED 179 133. 98 pp. MF–01; PC–04.

Ivancevich, J., and J. Donnelly. March 1968. "Job Satisfaction Research: A Manageable Guide for Practitioners." *Personnel Journal*
47: 172–77.

Jacobs, F. 1990. "Expectations of and by Faculty: An Overview for
the 1990s." In *An Agenda for the New Decade,* edited by L.W. Jones
and F.A. Nowotny. New Directions for Higher Education No. 70.
San Francisco: Jossey-Bass.

Jones, L. 1979. "Black Students Enrolled in White Colleges and Universities: Their Attitudes and Perceptions." Atlanta: Southern
Regional Education Board. ED 181 834. 34 pp. MF–01; PC–02.

Jones, L.W., and F.A. Nowotny, eds. 1990. *An Agenda for the New
Decade.* New Directions for Higher Education No. 70. San Francisco: Jossey-Bass.

Jones, S., and G. Weathersby. 1978. "Financing the Black College."
In *Black Colleges in America,* edited by C. Willie and R. Edmonds.
New York: Teachers College Press.

Justus, J.B., S.B. Freitag, and L.L. Parker. 1987. *The University of California in the Twenty-First Century: Successful Approaches to
Faculty Diversity.* Los Angeles: Univ. of California.

Kandel, D.B., M. Davies, and V.R. Raveis. 1985. "The Stressfulness
of Daily Social Roles for Women: Marital, Occupational, and Household Roles." *Journal of Health and Social Behavior* 26: 64–78.

Katzell, R. 1979. "Changing Attitudes toward Work." In *Work in Amer-*

ica: The Decade Ahead, edited by C. Kerr and J. Rosow. New York: Van Nostrand Reinhold.

Kulik, C., G.R. Oldham, and J. Hackman. 1987. "Work Design as an Approach to Person-Environment Fit." *Journal of Vocational Behavior* 31: 278–96.

Ladd, E., Jr. 1979. "The Work Experience of American College Professors: Some Data and an Argument." In *Faculty Career Development.* Current Issues in Higher Education No. 2. Paper read at an annual meeting of the American Association for Higher Education, Washington, D.C. ED 193 998. 44 pp. MF–01; PC not available EDRS.

LaFollette, W., and H. Sims, Jr. 1975. "Is Satisfaction Redundant with Organizational Climate?" *Organizational Behavior and Human Performance* 13: 257–78.

Landino, R., and L. Welch. 1990. "Supporting Women in the University Environment through Collaboration and Networking" In *Women in Higher Education: Changes and Challenges,* edited by L. B. Welch. New York: Praeger.

Lawler, E., III, and D. Hall. 1970. "Relationship of Job Characteristics to Job Involvement, Satisfaction, and Intrinsic Motivation." *Journal of Applied Psychology* 54: 305–12.

Leon, J. 1973. "An Investigation of the Applicability of the Two-Factor Theory of Job Satisfaction among College and University Professors." Ph.D. dissertation, Univ. of Arkansas.

Lewis, K.E., and M.M. Bierly. March–June 1986. "Sex Differences in Career Progression Strategies Preferred by University Faculty." *Group and Organization Studies* 11: 49–60.

Likert, R. 1961. *New Patterns of Management.* New York: McGraw-Hill.

Litwin, G., and R. Stringer. 1968. *Motivation and Organizational Climate.* Boston: Harvard Univ., Graduate School of Business Administration, Div. of Research.

Lloyd, S.A., et al. 1982. "Support Networks of Dual-Career Couples." Paper read at an annual meeting of the National Council on Family Relations, Washington, D.C. ED 228 590. 17 pp. MF–01; PC–01.

Locke, E. 1969. "What Is Job Satisfaction?" *Organizational Behavior and Human Performance* 4: 309–36.

———. 1973. "Satisfiers and Dissatisfiers among White-Collar and Blue-Collar Employees." *Journal of Applied Psychology* 58: 67–76.

———. 1976. "The Nature and Causes of Job Satisfaction." In *Handbook of Industrial and Organizational Psychology,* edited by M. Dunnette. Chicago: Rand McNally.

Locke, E., W. Fitzpatrick, and F. White. Summer 1983. "Job Satisfaction and Role Clarity among University and College Faculty." *Review of Higher Education* 6: 343–65.

Logan, C. 1990. "Job Satisfaction of African-American Faculty at Predominantly African-American and Predominantly White Four-Year, State-Assisted Institutions in the South." Ph.D. dissertation, Bowling Green State Univ.

Luu, H. 1985. "The Perceived Job Security and Job Satisfaction of Non-tenured Faculty Members." Ph.D. dissertation, Univ. of Houston.

"The Madison Plan." February 1988. Madison: Univ. of Wisconsin–Madison, Office of the Chancellor.

Maher, J. 1971. "Job Enrichment, Performance, and Morale in a Simulated Factory." In *New Perspectives in Job Enrichment,* edited by J. Maher. New York: Van Nostrand Reinhold.

Maitland, C. 1990. "The Inequitable Treatment of Women Faculty in Higher Education." In *Women in Higher Education: Changes and Challenges,* edited by L. B. Welch. New York: Praeger.

Marshall, M.R., and C.H. Jones. November 1990. "Childbearing Sequence and the Career Development of Women Administrators in Higher Education." *Journal of College Student Development* 31: 531–37.

Marwell, G., R. Rosenfeld, and S. Spelerman. 1979. "Geographic Constraints on Women's Careers in Academia." *Science* 205: 1225–31.

Maxwell, B. 1981. *Employment of Minority Ph.D.s: Changes over Time.* Washington, D.C.: National Research Council, Commission on Human Resources.

Mayfield, B., and W. Nash. 1976. "Career Attitudes of Female Professors." *Psychological Reports* 39: 631–34.

"Minorities in Higher Education." Summer 1992. *Department Chair* 3: 1–24.

"Minority Faculty Recruiting Pays Off." Fall 1990. *At BG* 20: 6.

Minority Resource Center. 1990. *Minority Resource Directory.* Detroit: University Counseling Services, Div. of Student Affairs.

Moore, K.M., and M.P. Johnson. 1989. "The Status of Women and Minorities in the Professoriate: The Role of Affirmative Action and Equity." In *Managing Faculty Resources,* edited by G.G. Lozier and M.J. Dooris. New Directions for Institutional Research No. 63. San Francisco: Jossey-Bass.

Moore, W., Jr., and L. Wagstaff. 1974. *Black Educators in White Colleges.* San Francisco: Jossey-Bass.

Morgan, J. 31 January 1991. "Accommodating the Trailing Spouse: Rules against Nepotism Take a Back Seat in Tight Market." *Black Issues in Higher Education* 7: 12–14.

Morse, N. 1953. *Satisfactions in White-Collar Jobs.* Ann Arbor: Univ. of Michigan, Institute for Social Research.

Moses, I. 1986. "Promotion of Academic Staff: Reward and Incentive." *Higher Education* 15: 135–49.

Murray, M. 1983. "Job Satisfaction and Job Dissatisfaction Experienced by Nurse-Faculty in Baccalaureate Nursing Programs." Ph.D. dissertation, Columbia Univ., Teachers College.

Naisbitt, J., and P. Aburdene. 1990. *Megatrends 2000: Ten New Directions for the 1990s.* New York: William Morrow & Co.

National Advisory Committee on Black Higher Education and Black Colleges and Universities. 1980. *Still a Lifeline: The Status of Historically Black Colleges and Universities.* Washington, D.C.: Author. ED 192 700. 79 pp. MF–01; PC–04.

National Urban League, Inc. 1982. "Tri-State Minority Faculty Employment Opportunity Project. Final Report." New York: Author. ED 236 261. 408 pp. MF–01; PC–17.

Near, J.P., and M.D. Sorcinelli. 1986. "Work and Life away from Work: Predictors of Faculty Satisfaction." *Research in Higher Education* 25: 377–94.

Neely, J. 1981. "A Study of Socialization and Job Satisfaction of Faculty at an Urban Two-year Community College." Ph.D. dissertation, Ohio State Univ.

Newell, L., and K. Spear. 1983. "New Dimensions for Academic Careers: Rediscovering Intrinsic Satisfactions." *Liberal Education* 69: 109–16.

Nicholson, E., and R. Miljus. November 1972. "Job Satisfaction and Turnover among Liberal Arts College Professors." *Personnel Journal* 51: 840–45.

Nieves-Squires, S. 1991. "Hispanic Women: Making Their Presence on Campus Less Tenuous." Washington, D.C.: Association of American Colleges. ED 334 907. 16 pp. MF–01; PC–01.

Nussel, E., W. Wiersma, and P. Rusche. May/June 1988. "Work Satisfaction of Education Professors." *Journal of Teacher Education* 39: 45–50.

Office of Instructional Research and Planning Analysis. February 1990. *An Analysis of the Black Instructional Faculty and Administrators Satisfaction Survey.* Blacksburg: Virginia Polytechnic Institute and State Univ.

Patchen, M. 1961. *The Choice of Wage Comparisons.* Englewood Cliffs, N.J.: Prentice-Hall.

———. 1970. *Participation, Achievement, and Involvement on the Job.* Englewood Cliffs, N.J.: Prentice-Hall.

Payne, N. September/October 1989. "Hidden Messages in the Pursuit of Equality." *Academe* 75: 19–22.

Pearlin, L.I., and C. Schooler. March 1978. "The Structure of Coping." *Journal of Health and Social Behavior* 19: 2–21.

Pearson, D., and R. Seiler. 1983. "Environmental Satisfiers in Academe." *Higher Education* 12: 35–47.

Pelz, D., and F. Andrews. 1976. *Scientists in Organizations.* New York: John Wiley & Sons.

Peterson, S. 1990. "Challenges for Black Women Faculty." *Initiatives* 53 (Special Issue: Black Women in Higher Education): 33–36.

Pfeffer, J., and J. Lawler. March 1980. "Effects of Job Alternatives, Extrinsic Rewards, and Behavioral Commitment on Attitude toward the Organization: A Field Test of the Insufficient Justification Paradigm." *Administrative Science Quarterly* 25: 38–56.

"Ph.D.s for Women Up, More Leave Academe." 10 September 1990. *Higher Education and National Affairs* 39: 4.

Plascak-Craig, F., and J. Bean. 1989. "Education Faculty Job Satisfaction in Major Research Universities." Paper read at an annual meeting of the Association for the Study of Higher Education, Atlanta, Georgia. ED 313 987. 31 pp. MF–01; PC–02.

Porter, L., and R. Steers. 1973. "Organizational, Work, and Personal Factors in Employee Turnover and Absenteeism." *Psychological Bulletin* 80: 151–76.

Powell, J., E. Barrett, and V. Shanker. 1983. "How Academics View Their Work." *Higher Education* 12: 297–313.

Rafky, D. December 1972. "The Black Scholar in the Academic Marketplace." *Teachers College Record* 74: 225–60.

"Recruiting Minority Faculty: Two Success Stories." 12 November 1990. *Administrator* 9: 1–2.

Rempel, A., and R. Bentley. Winter 1970. "Teacher Morale: Relationship with Selected Factors." *Journal of Teacher Education* 21: 534–39.

Reskin, B.F., and P.A. Phipps. 1988. "Women in Male-Dominated Professional and Managerial Occupations." In *Women Working*, edited by A.H. Stromberg and S. Harkess. 2d rev. ed. Mountain View, Calif.: Mayfield Publishing Co.

Sagaria, M.A. 1988. "Administrative Mobility and Gender: Patterns and Processes in Higher Education." *Journal of Higher Education* 59: 305–28.

Saleb, S.D., and M. Lalljee. 1969. "Sex and Job Orientation." *Personnel Psychology* 22: 465–71.

Sanders, K.W., and G.O. Mellow. 1990. "Permanent Diversity: The Deferred Vision of Higher Education." *Initiatives* 53 (Special Issue: Black Women in Higher Education): 9–13.

Saunders, D. 12 April 1990. "Tenure for Black Faculty: An Illusion in the White Academy." *Black Issues in Higher Education* 7: 32.

Scarr, S., D. Phillips, and K. McCartney. November 1989. "Working Mothers and Their Families." *American Psychologist* 44: 1402–9.

Schultz, J.B., and Y.L. Chung. 1988. "Research Productivity and Job Satisfaction of University Faculty." *Journal of Vocational Education Research* 13: 33–48.

Schuster, J.H. December 1986. "The Faculty Dilemma: A Short Course." *Phi Delta Kappan* 68: 275–82.

———. 1990. "Faculty Issues in the 1990s: New Realities, New Opportunities." In *An Agenda for the New Decade,* edited by L.W. Jones and F.A. Nowotny. New Directions for Higher Education No. 70. San Francisco: Jossey-Bass.

Seeborg, I.S. 1990. "Division of Labor in Two-Career Faculty Households." In *Women in Higher Education: Changes and Challenges,* edited by L. B. Welch. New York: Praeger.

Seegmiller, J. 1977. "Job Satisfaction of Faculty and Staff at the College of Eastern Utah." Price: College of Eastern Utah. ED 139 489. 40 pp. MF–01; PC–02.

Seidman, P. 10 September 1990a. "52 New Minority Faculty Hired: 2nd Record Year." *University Record* 46: 1+.

———. 5 February 1990b. "University Builds Links with Black, Hispanic Colleges." *University Record* 45: 1.

Sekaran, U. 1986. *Dual-Career Families: Contemporary Organizational and Counseling Issues.* San Francisco: Jossey-Bass.

Sheppard, H., and N. Herrick. 1972. *Where Have All the Robots Gone? Worker Dissatisfaction in the '70s.* New York: Free Press.

Sherman, S.R., R.A. Ward, and M. LaGory. 1988. "Women as Caregivers of the Elderly: Instrumental and Expressive Support." *Social Work* 33: 164–68.

Silver, J., R. Dennis, and C. Spikes. 1988. *Black Faculty in Traditionally White Institutions in Selected Adams States: Characteristics, Experiences, and Perceptions.* Atlanta: Southern Education Foundation. ED 299 891. 151 pp. MF–01; PC–07.

Simeone, A. 1987. *Academic Women: Working towards Equality.* South Hadley, Mass.: Bergin & Garvey.

Smith, E., and T. Zorn. 1981. "Educational Equity: Results of a National Survey to Identify the Nature and Extent of Discrimination Perceived by Black Students and Advocates in Postsecondary Institutions." Paper read at an annual meeting of the American Educational Research Association, Los Angeles, California. ED 205 637. 16 pp. MF–01; PC–01.

Smith, J., D. Simpson-Kirkland, J. Zimmeren, E. Goldenstein, and K. Prichard. April 1986. "The Five Most Important Problems Confronting Black Students Today." *Negro Educational Review* 37: 52–61.

Sorcinelli, M.D., and J.P. Near. January/February 1989. "Relations between Work and Life away from Work among University Faculty." *Journal of Higher Education* 60: 59–81.

Sprague, B. 1974. "Job Satisfaction and University Faculty." Ph.D. dissertation, Univ. of Kentucky.

Stafford, S.G., and G.B. Spanier. 1990. "Recruiting the Dual-Career Couple: The Family Employment Program." *Initiatives* 53: 37–44.

Staples, R. March/April 1984. "Racial Ideology and Intellectual Racism: Blacks in Academia." *Black Scholar* 15: 2–17.

Steen, J., L. Giunipero, and K. Newgren. May 1985. "A Profile of Management Faculty: Teaching, Research, and Career Satisfaction." *Journal of Business Education* 60: 347–52.

Stern, C.S. September/October 1990. "Time Past and Time Future: A 75th Anniversary Address." *Academe* 76: 47–52.

Steward, R. 1987. "Work Satisfaction and the Black Female Professional: A Pilot Study." Lawrence: Univ. of Kansas. ED 316 766. 12

pp. MF–01; PC–01.

Stogdill, R., and A. Coons, eds. 1957. *Leader Behavior: Its Description and Measurement.* Columbus: Ohio State Univ., Bureau of Business Research.

Stoner, J. 1982. *Management.* 2d rev. ed. Englewood Cliffs, N.J.: Prentice-Hall.

Teevan, J., S. Pepper, and J. Pellizzari. 1992. "Academic Employment Decisions and Gender." *Research in Higher Education* 33: 141–57.

Theodore, A. 1971. "The Professional Woman: Trends and Prospects." In *The Professional Woman,* edited by A. Theodore. Cambridge, Mass.: Schenkman Publishing Co.

Thoits, P.A. April 1983. "Multiple Identities and Psychological Well-Being." *American Sociological Review* 48: 174–87.

Thoreson, R.W., C.M. Kardash, D.A. Leuthold, and K.A. Morow. 1990. "Gender Differences in Academic Careers." *Research in Higher Education* 31: 193–209.

Toombs, W., and J. Marlier. 1981. "Career Change among Academics: Dimensions of Decision." Paper read at an annual meeting of the American Educational Research Association, Los Angeles, California. ED 202 423. 40 pp. MF–01; PC–02.

U.S. Dept. of Education. 1990. *Faculty in Higher Education, 1988.* NCES Publication No. 90-365. Washington, D.C.: National Center for Education Statistics, Office of Educational Research and Improvement.

———. 1991. *Digest of Education Statistics.* Washington D.C.: National Center for Education Statistics, Office of Educational Research and Improvement. ED 340 141. 477 pp. MF–01; PC–20.

Vatthaisong, A. 1982. "A Study of Job Satisfaction and Dissatisfaction among Faculty Members in Teacher Training Institutions in Thailand." Ph.D. dissertation, Vanderbilt Univ., George Peabody College for Teachers.

Verbrugge, L.M. March 1983. "Multiple Roles and Physical Health of Women and Men." *Journal of Health and Social Behavior* 24: 16–30.

Villadsen, A.W., and M.W. Tack. 1981. "Combining Home and Career Responsibilities: The Methods Used by Women Executives in Higher Education." *Journal of the National Association of Women Deans, Administrators, and Counselors* 45: 20–25.

"Visiting Professors Program." 1988–89. *The University of Michigan King/Chavez/Parks (KCP) Yearbook.* Ann Arbor: Univ. of Michigan, Office of Minority Affairs.

Vontress, C. 1971. *Counseling Negroes.* New York: Houghton Mifflin.

Vroom, V. 1964. *Work and Motivation.* New York: John Wiley & Sons.

Washington, V., and W. Harvey. 1989. *Affirmative Rhetoric, Negative Action: African-American and Hispanic Faculty at Predominantly White Institutions.* ASHE-ERIC Higher Education Report No. 2. Washington, D.C.: George Washington Univ., School of Education and Human Development. ED 316 075. 128 pp. MF–01; PC–06.

Weaver, C.N. June 1974. "Sex Differences in Job Satisfaction." *Business Horizons* 17: 43–49.

Weick, K. 1966. "The Concept of Equity in the Perception of Pay." *Administrative Science Quarterly* 11: 414–39.

Willie, R., and J. Stecklein. 1982. "A Three-Decade Comparison of College Faculty Characteristics, Satisfactions, Activities, and Attitudes." *Research in Higher Education* 16: 81–93.

Wilson, B., and E. Byrne. 1987. *Women in the University: A Policy Report.* St. Lucia, Queensland: Univ. of Queensland Press.

Wilson, R. February 1987. "Recruitment and Retention of Minority Faculty and Staff." *AAHE Bulletin* 39: 11–14.

Wilson, R. and D. Carter. 1988. *Minorities in Higher Education: Seventh Annual Status Report.* Washington, D.C.: American Council on Education.

Wilson, R., and S. Melendez. Fall 1985. "Down the Up Staircase." *Educational Record* 66: 46–50.

———. 1986. *Minorities in Higher Education: Fifth Annual Status Report.* Washington, D.C.: American Council on Education.

Wilson, R., L. Woods, and J. Gaff. Winter 1974. "Social-Psychological Accessibility and Faculty-Student Interaction beyond the Classroom." *Sociology of Education* 47: 74–92.

Winfield, F. 1987. "Workplace Solutions for Women under Eldercare Pressure." *Personnel* 64: 31–39.

Winkler, L. 1982. "Job Satisfaction of University Faculty in the U.S." Ph.D. dissertation, Univ. of Nebraska.

Wissman, J. 1981. "The Effect of Faculty Gender on Job Satisfaction in Selected Sex-Typed Units within Institutions of Higher Education." Ph.D. dissertation, Univ. of Kansas.

———. 1988. "Job Satisfaction in a Divided Academy." *Initiatives* 51: 39–43.

Wolfson, R. 1986. "Job Satisfaction of Industrial Arts/Technology Teacher Education Faculty in the United States." Ph.D. dissertation, Ohio State Univ.

Yuker, H. 1984. *Faculty Workload: Research, Theory, and Interpretation.* ASHE-ERIC Higher Education Report No. 10. Washington, D.C.: Association for the Study of Higher Education. ED 259 691. 120 pp. MF–01; PC–05.

INDEX

A

Achievement & recognition, 15-16, 37
African-American faculty
    attitudes & perceptions, 61, 68
    job satisfaction, 35, 59-60
    numbers of, 55
    racial climate, 70-72
    rank enumeration, 64
    representation in disciplines, 33
    salaries, 60-62
    supervision, 70
    tenure, 62-64, 66
    working conditions, 41
    work environment, 68-70
Asian faculty
    numbers of, 2, 55
    representation in disciplines, 33
    tenure, 65

B

Bowling Green State University
    diversification incentives, 94-95

C

Center for Minority Staff Development, 85
Child care, 91-92
Collective Bargaining
    affecting job satisfaction, 29-31

D

Diversification incentives programs, 92-96
Doctoral degrees
    earned by minorities, 34
    earned by women, 34

E

ERIC system, 6

F

Faculty in future
    salaries more significant, 2
    will be inadequate, 1-2
    remain dedicated ?, 3-4
Family demands, 44-46
Family Employment Program (FEP), 90-91

H

Herzberg's theory of job satisfaction, 6

Hispanic faculty
        ennumeration by rank, 65
        number of, 2, 55
        racial climate, 73
        representation in disciplines, 33
        teaching, 36
        tenure, 65, 67
        work environment, 69

I

Institutional support, 89
Interaction between students & teachers, 13
Interpersonal relationships, 40-41
        affecting job satisfaction, 26-27

J

Job referral support, 91
Job satisfaction, 34, 35, 59-60
        internal stress factors, 9-18
        literature, 5-6, 7-8, 58-59

L

Long Beach City College
        diversification incentives, 95-96

M

Marriage and children
        child care, 49-50
        commuting marriage, 47-48, 89
        dual-career families, 46-47
        elder care, 50
        health, 50-52
        household responsibilities, 48-49
        multiple roles, 50-51
Meaningful faculty work activities, 9
Mentor relationship, 85-86
Merit systems, 21-22
Miami University of Ohio
        diversification incentives, 93
Minority faculty
        discussion of, 55-74
        interpersonal relationships, 40-41
        need for, 55-58
        numbers of, 2, 55
        representation in disciplines, 33
        salary preference, 91
        tenure, 62, 65
Motivation needs, 29

N

Native American Faculty
numbers of, 2, 55
representation in disciplines, 33
tenure, 65
Nepotism laws on campus, 89-90
Networking promotion, 83-86

P

Person-Environment Fit
affecting job satisfaction, 28-29
Policies and Administration
affecting job satisfaction, 27-28
Promotion & growth, 16-17
Psycinfo system, 6

Q

Quality of the students, 12

R

Racial climate, 70-73
Rank
affecting job satisfaction, 24-25
enumeration, 64-65
Recruiting & Retaining, 75-99
ABD (all but dissertation), 81
assistantships, 78
faculty exchange, 79-81
fellowships, 78, 80
hiring own graduates, 79
need for long term plans, 76-77
participation in projects, 77
strategies for recruitment, 76
Reduction of inequity methods, 20
Research, 10, 54
Reputation of colleagues, 11-12
Requirements, 11

S

Salaries, 38-39, 91
academic decline, 2
affecting job satisfaction, 19-22
Southern Association of Colleges and Schools
accreditation region, 58
SUNY system
diversification incentives, 92-93
Supervision
affecting job satisfaction, 25-26

T

Target of Opportunity Fund, 95
Targets of Opportunity Program (TOP), 92
Teaching, 10, 36
Tenure
        by academic rank , 23
        by sex, 24
        childbirth privileges, 86-87
        criteria defined, 87- 88
        affecting job satisfaction, 22-24
        publications requirement, 66
        research support, 87-88
        service criteria, 66-67

U

Underrepresented Faculty Initiative, 92-93
University of California
        diversification incentives, 92
University of Michigan
        diversification incentives, 95
University of Minnesota
        tenure & security study, 23
University of Wisconsin-Madison,
        diversification incentives, 94

V

Voluntary Affirmative Action Plan, 93

W

Wayne State University
        diversification incentives, 95
Woman Faculty, 33-52
        achievement & recognition, 37
        interpersonal relationships, 40
        job discrimination, 35
        job satisfaction, 34
        marriage & children, 46
        numbers, 2, 55
        rank, 39-40
        representation in disciplines, 33
        salaries, 38-39, 91
        teaching, 36
        tenure, 39
        working conditions, 41-42
        work load, 43-44
Working conditions, 41-42
        affecting job satisfaction, 27
Work environment, 67-70

Work load
    of academics, 42-44

ASHE-ERIC HIGHER EDUCATION REPORTS

Since 1983, the Association for the Study of Higher Education (ASHE) and the Educational Resources Information Center (ERIC) Clearinghouse on Higher Education, a sponsored project of the School of Education and Human Development at The George Washington University, have cosponsored the *ASHE-ERIC Higher Education Report* series. The 1992 series is the twenty-first overall and the fourth to be published by the School of Education and Human Development at the George Washington University.

Each monograph is the definitive analysis of a tough higher education problem, based on thorough research of pertinent literature and institutional experiences. Topics are identified by a national survey. Noted practitioners and scholars are then commissioned to write the reports, with experts providing critical reviews of each manuscript before publication.

Eight monographs (10 before 1985) in the ASHE-ERIC Higher Education Report series are published each year and are available on individual and subscription bases. Subscription to eight issues is $90.00 annually; $70 to members of AAHE, AIR, or AERA; and $60 to ASHE members. All foreign subscribers must include an additional $10 per series year for postage.

To order single copies of existing reports, use the order form on the last page of this book. Regular prices, and special rates available to members of AAHE, AIR, AERA and ASHE, are as follows:

Series	Regular	Members
1990 to 92	$17.00	$12.75
1988 and 89	15.00	11.25
1985 to 87	10.00	7.50
1983 and 84	7.50	6.00
before 1983	6.50	5.00

Price includes book rate postage within the U.S. For foreign orders, please add $1.00 per book. Fast United Parcel Service available within the contiguous U.S. at $2.50 for each order under $50.00, and calculated at 5% of invoice total for orders $50.00 or above.

All orders under $45.00 must be prepaid. Make check payable to ASHE-ERIC. For Visa or MasterCard, include card number, expiration date and signature. A bulk discount of 10% is available on orders of 10 or more books, and 40% on orders of 25 or more books (not applicable on subscriptions).

Address order to
ASHE-ERIC Higher Education Reports
The George Washington University
1 Dupont Circle, Suite 630
Washington, DC 20036
Or phone (202) 296-2597
Write or call for a complete catalog.

1992 ASHE-ERIC Higher Education Reports

1. The Leadership Compass: Values and Ethics in Higher Education
John R. Wilcox and Susan L. Ebbs

2. Preparing for a Global Community: Achieving an International Perspective in Higher Education
Sarah M. Pickert

3. Quality: Transforming Postsecondary Education
Ellen Earle Chaffee and Lawrence A. Sherr

1991 ASHE-ERIC Higher Education Reports

1. Active Learning: Creating Excitement in the Classroom
Charles C. Bonwell and James A. Eison

2. Realizing Gender Equality in Higher Education: The Need to Integrate Work/Family Issues
Nancy Hensel

3. Academic Advising for Student Success: A System of Shared Responsibility
Susan H. Frost

4. Cooperative Learning: Increasing College Faculty Instructional Productivity
David W. Johnson, Roger T. Johnson, and Karl A. Smith

5. High School–College Partnerships: Conceptual Models, Programs, and Issues
Arthur Richard Greenberg

6. Meeting the Mandate: Renewing the College and Departmental Curriculum
William Toombs and William Tierney

7. Faculty Collaboration: Enhancing the Quality of Scholarship and Teaching
Ann E. Austin and Roger G. Baldwin

8. Strategies and Consequences: Managing the Costs in Higher Education
John S. Waggaman

1990 ASHE-ERIC Higher Education Reports

1. The Campus Green: Fund Raising in Higher Education
Barbara E. Brittingham and Thomas R. Pezzullo

2. The Emeritus Professor: Old Rank - New Meaning
James E. Mauch, Jack W. Birch, and Jack Matthews

3. "High Risk" Students in Higher Education: Future Trends
Dionne J. Jones and Betty Collier Watson

4. Budgeting for Higher Education at the State Level: Enigma, Paradox, and Ritual
   Daniel T. Layzell and Jan W. Lyddon

5. Proprietary Schools: Programs, Policies, and Prospects
   John B. Lee and Jamie P. Merisotis

6. College Choice: Understanding Student Enrollment Behavior
   Michael B. Paulsen

7. Pursuing Diversity: Recruiting College Minority Students
   Barbara Astone and Elsa Nuñez-Wormack

8. Social Consciousness and Career Awareness: Emerging Link in Higher Education
   John S. Swift, Jr.

1989 ASHE-ERIC Higher Education Reports

1. Making Sense of Administrative Leadership: The 'L' Word in Higher Education
   Estela M. Bensimon, Anna Neumann, and Robert Birnbaum

2. Affirmative Rhetoric, Negative Action: African-American and Hispanic Faculty at Predominantly White Universities
   Valora Washington and William Harvey

3. Postsecondary Developmental Programs: A Traditional Agenda with New Imperatives
   Louise M. Tomlinson

4. The Old College Try: Balancing Athletics and Academics in Higher Education
   John R. Thelin and Lawrence L. Wiseman

5. The Challenge of Diversity: Involvement or Alienation in the Academy?
   Daryl G. Smith

6. Student Goals for College and Courses: A Missing Link in Assessing and Improving Academic Achievement
   Joan S. Stark, Kathleen M. Shaw, and Malcolm A. Lowther

7. The Student as Commuter: Developing a Comprehensive Institutional Response
   Barbara Jacoby

8. Renewing Civic Capacity: Preparing College Students for Service and Citizenship
   Suzanne W. Morse

1988 ASHE-ERIC Higher Education Reports

1. The Invisible Tapestry: Culture in American Colleges and Universities
   George D. Kuh and Elizabeth J. Whitt

2. Critical Thinking: Theory, Research, Practice, and Possibilities
   Joanne Gainen Kurfiss

3. Developing Academic Programs: The Climate for Innovation
   Daniel T. Seymour

4. Peer Teaching: To Teach is To Learn Twice
   Neal A. Whitman

5. Higher Education and State Governments: Renewed Partnership, Cooperation, or Competition?
   Edward R. Hines

6. Entrepreneurship and Higher Education: Lessons for Colleges, Universities, and Industry
   James S. Fairweather

7. Planning for Microcomputers in Higher Education: Strategies for the Next Generation
   Reynolds Ferrante, John Hayman, Mary Susan Carlson, and Harry Phillips

8. The Challenge for Research in Higher Education: Harmonizing Excellence and Utility
   Alan W. Lindsay and Ruth T. Neumann

1987 ASHE-ERIC Higher Education Reports

1. Incentive Early Retirement Programs for Faculty: Innovative Responses to a Changing Environment
   Jay L. Chronister and Thomas R. Kepple, Jr.

2. Working Effectively with Trustees: Building Cooperative Campus Leadership
   Barbara E. Taylor

3. Formal Recognition of Employer-Sponsored Instruction: Conflict and Collegiality in Postsecondary Education
   Nancy S. Nash and Elizabeth M. Hawthorne

4. Learning Styles: Implications for Improving Educational Practices
   Charles S. Claxton and Patricia H. Murrell

5. Higher Education Leadership: Enhancing Skills through Professional Development Programs
   Sharon A. McDade

6. Higher Education and the Public Trust: Improving Stature in Colleges and Universities
   Richard L. Alfred and Julie Weissman

7. College Student Outcomes Assessment: A Talent Development Perspective
   Maryann Jacobi, Alexander Astin, and Frank Ayala, Jr.

8. Opportunity from Strength: Strategic Planning Clarified with Case Examples
   Robert G. Cope

1986 ASHE-ERIC Higher Education Reports

1. Post-tenure Faculty Evaluation: Threat or Opportunity?
   Christine M. Licata

2. Blue Ribbon Commissions and Higher Education: Changing Academe from the Outside
   Janet R. Johnson and Laurence R. Marcus

3. Responsive Professional Education: Balancing Outcomes and Opportunities
   Joan S. Stark, Malcolm A. Lowther, and Bonnie M.K. Hagerty

4. Increasing Students' Learning: A Faculty Guide to Reducing Stress among Students
   Neal A. Whitman, David C. Spendlove, and Claire H. Clark

5. Student Financial Aid and Women: Equity Dilemma?
   Mary Moran

6. The Master's Degree: Tradition, Diversity, Innovation
   Judith S. Glazer

7. The College, the Constitution, and the Consumer Student: Implications for Policy and Practice
   Robert M. Hendrickson and Annette Gibbs

8. Selecting College and University Personnel: The Quest and the Question
   Richard A. Kaplowitz

1985 ASHE-ERIC Higher Education Reports

1. Flexibility in Academic Staffing: Effective Policies and Practices
   Kenneth P. Mortimer, Marque Bagshaw, and Andrew T. Masland

2. Associations in Action: The Washington, D.C. Higher Education Community
   Harland G. Bloland

3. And on the Seventh Day: Faculty Consulting and Supplemental Income
   Carol M. Boyer and Darrell R. Lewis

4. Faculty Research Performance: Lessons from the Sciences and Social Sciences
   John W. Creswell

5. Academic Program Review: Institutional Approaches, Expectations, and Controversies
   Clifton F. Conrad and Richard F. Wilson

6. Students in Urban Settings: Achieving the Baccalaureate Degree
   Richard C. Richardson, Jr. and Louis W. Bender

7. Serving More Than Students: A Critical Need for College Student
   Personnel Services
   Peter H. Garland

8. Faculty Participation in Decision Making: Necessity or Luxury?
   Carol E. Floyd

1984 ASHE-ERIC Higher Education Reports

1. Adult Learning: State Policies and Institutional Practices
   K. Patricia Cross and Anne-Marie McCartan

2. Student Stress: Effects and Solutions
   Neal A. Whitman, David C. Spendlove, and Claire H. Clark

3. Part-time Faulty: Higher Education at a Crossroads
   Judith M. Gappa

4. Sex Discrimination Law in Higher Education: The Lessons of
   the Past Decade. ED 252 169.*
   *J. Ralph Lindgren, Patti T. Ota, Perry A. Zirkel, and Nan Van
   Gieson*

5. Faculty Freedoms and Institutional Accountability: Interactions
   and Conflicts
   Steven G. Olswang and Barbara A. Lee

6. The High Technology Connection: Academic/Industrial Cooperation for Economic Growth
   Lynn G. Johnson

7. Employee Educational Programs: Implications for Industry and
   Higher Education. ED 258 501.*
   Suzanne W. Morse

8. Academic Libraries: The Changing Knowledge Centers of Colleges and Universities
   Barbara B. Moran

9. Futures Research and the Strategic Planning Process: Implications for Higher Education
   James L. Morrison, William L. Renfro, and Wayne I. Boucher

10. Faculty Workload: Research, Theory, and Interpretation
    Harold E. Yuker

*Out-of-print. Available through EDRS. Call 1-800-443-ERIC.

Quantity **Amount**

_____ Please begin my subscription to the 1992 *ASHE-ERIC Higher Education Reports* at $90.00, 33% off the cover price, starting with Report 1, 1992. _____

_____ Please send a complete set of the 1991 *ASHE-ERIC Higher Education Reports* at $80.00, 41% off the cover price. _____

_____ Outside the U.S., add $10.00 per series for postage. _____

Individual reports are avilable at the following prices:

1990 and 1991, $17.00	1983 and 1984, $7.50
1988 and 1989, $15.00	1982 and back, $6.50
1985 to 1987, $10.00	

Book rate postage within the U.S. is included. Outside U.S., please add $1.00 per book for postage. Fast U.P.S. shipping is available within the contiguous U.S. at $2.50 for each order under $50.00, and calculated at 5% of invoice total for orders $50.00 or above. All orders under $45.00 must be prepaid.

PLEASE SEND ME THE FOLLOWING REPORTS:

Quantity	Report No.	Year	Title	Amount

Subtotal:	
Foreign or UPS:	
Total Due:	

Please check one of the following:
☐ Check enclosed, payable to GWU–ERIC.
☐ Purchase order attached ($45.00 minimum).
☐ Charge my credit card indicated below:
   ☐ Visa   ☐ MasterCard

Expiration Date _____

Name _____

Title _____

Institution _____

Address _____

City _____ State _____ Zip _____

Phone _____

Signature _____ Date _____

SEND ALL ORDERS TO:
ASHE-ERIC Higher Education Reports
The George Washington University
One Dupont Circle, Suite 630
Washington, DC 20036-1183
Phone: (202) 296-2597